THE CARE
AND
MAINTENANCE
OF
small boats

THE CARE
AND
MAINTENANCE
OF small boats
Donald Cantin

DRAKE PUBLISHERS INC.
New York

623.8
C

Published in 1973 by
Drake Publishers Inc.
381 Park Avenue South
New York, N.Y. 10016

Copyright © by Drake Publishers Inc.,1973

Library of Congress Cataloging in Publication Data
Cantin, Donald W.
The care and maintenance of small boats.
1. Boats and boating—Maintenance and repair.

I. Title.
VM321.C28   623.82'02   73-4786
ISBN 0-87749-500-9

Printed in the United States of America

Prepared and produced for the publisher by BMG Productions,
Incorporated

c.2

Dedicated to all past, present, and future members of the Halloween Yacht Club, Stamford, Connecticut.

contents

ACKNOWLEDGEMENTS

I hate to admit it, but I'm partially responsible for this book.

Not too long ago, the author and I were racing aboard my Cottontail "Wabbit" off Stamford, Conn. I was skipper, with Don as crew (the important 60 percent of the team—the crew has to *work* on a Cottontail). The wind was a steady Southeaster—12 to 15—and we got a perfect start. We hit the weather end of the line right at the gun—beautiful! Don nodded his approval and hiked—hard.

We tacked over the fleet and were off in the lead with clear air. Duck Soup. First around the weather mark, just ahead of the pack. And just barely ahead again at the leeward pin. Don doused the chute and pulled all the right strings, and we sheeted in for the beat back to the finish. I hiked while he hooked onto the trapeze "wire" and swung out to keep "Wabbit" flat and driving.

Suddenly we righted, came up into the wind —sails flogging and snapping—and stayed there.

The fleet went by as if we were standing still. We were completely out of control—and drifting *backwards*!

"What the #!?&#¢@%! did you do?" I yelled at Don—politely. It *had* to be *his* fault—*I* hadn't done anything wrong!

He didn't deign to answer. Just raised his arm and pointed aft. There was a glimpse of something white awash in the waves. Our rudder had busted off—and was floating gently astern.

We not only lost the race; we never even finished. Just picked up the rudder, then sailed back to the club steering with a paddle over the transom.

I strongly suspect that it was on that very day that Don decided that the boat world needed this book.

I'm insulted. Is he trying to tell me—a performance sailor—that a little preventive maintenance could have kept the fittings on my rudder from working loose? That we could—in fact should—have won that race?

Read on. And, hopefully, never leave your rudder astern.

Reg Page

National Champion,
International Cottontail Class

introduction

The care and maintenance of your boat is a matter of life and death.

If you've been a sailor or powerboatman for any length of time, you already know this to be a fact. If you're just getting into the sport, you can either take my word for it or find out the hard way.

I found out the hard way.

Not too long ago I thought I knew all about the care and maintenance of my boat. And why not? I had studied naval architecture; I had helped friends commission their boats; I had designed and built my own sailboat (25′ from bowsprit to clew outhaul). I thought I knew every nook and cranny aboard; she's husky, deliberately overbuilt for strength; a coat of paint in the spring is all she'll ever need.

Then one bright, sunlit afternoon, cutting along with fifteen knots across the beam, a freak, unannounced storm hit us. We saw the dark water ripples rapidly approaching from the distance, but my wife and I thought they were nothing more than cat's paws . . . localized gusts.

Wrong! It turned out to be a four-day storm. It hit us at forty knots, slamming the boat on its side, ripping the battens out of their pockets, then pulling the sail from the boom. The boat flipped over on its side and would have capsized if we hadn't cut the jib sheets. (I had fastened them wrong on the cleat and couldn't undo them against the pressure of the wind.) I wrapped the remains of my sail around the boom, pulled the jibs down, and bunched them up at the bow on their stays. Bad luck, I thought, but I still have my outboard motor and we'll get home on that.

Wrong again. The motor wouldn't kick over. I checked the fuel line. Fuel OK. I checked the plugs. Spark OK. I checked the prop. Nothing jamming it. So I swore a lot and pulled the starting cord until my fingers literally bled.

Four hours later and still miles from shore, we were soaking wet and being blown out to sea. The wind was still at forty knots with gusts to sixty. Swells had built to about seven feet. I improvised a sea anchor of cushions, a poncho, and a hank of rope, but it didn't do much good. The temperature had dropped thirty degrees.

Finally a police boat saw us and towed us in. Three hours later I was still shaking. (I get nervous now, just writing about it.)

Would proper "care and maintenance" have made any difference in a situation like this? I think so.

First, the sails were of Egyptian cotton and years

of use had weakened them. They should have been replaced long ago with new Dacron sails and with an extra row of reef points. This would have let me fly a "half-size" sail and might've let me sail out of that fix. I should have replaced the old-fashioned wooden cleats with fast-release jam cleats. Then I wouldn't have had to cut my jib sheets to keep from capsizing.

The engine trouble? In my haste to leave earlier in the day I had measured the oil-to-gas ratio improperly and had an oil-rich mixture that simply wouldn't fire. Also, in my panic, I'm sure I flooded the motor more than once.

I should have had the life jackets more accessible. Buoyant cushions are a nice extra measure of protection, but awkward as hell in a real emergency.

A real sea anchor instead of the jerry-rigged device I put together would've kept the bow more into the waves. Without it we took everything broadside and were really slapped around.

An International Orange distress flag and flares should have been aboard. Foul-weather gear for everyone would have kept us dryer and more comfortable. Some type of radio equipment for sending a MAYDAY signal would've been nice. It's expensive, but cheaper than a funeral.

This isn't an extreme example. I've heard dozens of stories where lives were endangered because the owner had put off minor repairs or had failed to provide proper safety equipment. Care and maintenance go beyond having a good-looking boat for others to admire ... or sprucing up when you're about to sell your boat in order to get a good price. You can have a safe and enjoyable boat that will be the envy of your guests and fellow boatmen with very little effort on your part.

Keeping your boat up needn't be looked upon as a chore. There are two simple things to keep in mind.

A) Have a positive attitude about working on your boat. If you approach it right, getting your boat ready can be as much fun as being out on the water. Get your family and friends involved; make a day or weekend event of it. Have refreshments available; follow up the work with play; have a barbecue for those who helped out. When your boat is ready to launch, have everyone who helped come along for a ride.

B) Practice something the army calls "preventive maintenance." Don't let minor problems become big chores. Periodically give your boat a visual checkover. Don't let a small hairline crack in your fiberglass hull become a tearing hole when you're miles from shore. Don't let a small area of soft, spongy wood on your boat become raging dry rot that will require replacing vital timbers. Don't let corrosion build up on metal parts until the day comes when your engine won't start, your radio gear won't transmit, or your flashlight won't light. Don't let your

lines go until they're so frayed they'd be useless in an emergency.

Although this book is "encyclopedic" in approach,
covering many areas in which you might have very
little interest (such as the sailboat chapter, if you're
a powerboatman), I recommend reading it all the
way through and not skipping around. You may not
have a stove aboard right now or an inflatable boat,
but reading the text on these subjects will help you
select the suitable equipment when the time comes.

If you're into boating enough to be reading this
book on care and maintenance, chances are you've
got a "commitment" to water sports that will last
you a lifetime. Of the more than sixty-three million
households in this country, almost one out of ten
has a boat of some kind. A recent survey by *Motor
Boating and Sailing* magazine indicated that almost
thirty percent of their subscribers owned two boats
and thirteen percent owned three boats!

You probably have heard the old joke that a boat
is a hole in the water surrounded by wood (or fiberglass) into which you throw money. Nevertheless,
once the water bug bites you the chances are you'll
be involved with boats for the rest of your life.
Whether your interest is fishing, cruising, racing,
water skiing, or scuba diving, the statistics show
that you will upgrade your boat and get a bigger
one, that you'll continue to add more and more
equipment aboard, and that you'll become a better
boatman.

You'll want to know how to select and care for your compass, head, galley, fire extinguishers, depth finders, radio telephone, and countless other items. The survey mentioned above reports that 36.8 percent of boat owners do *all* of their own maintenance . . . and 44 percent do part of it. *Rudder* magazine did a similar survey among its subscribers and found that 61.7 percent of boat owners did all their own maintenance work.

With almost six million registered crafts in the United States, that represents a great deal of owner maintenance. There are approximately one and one-half million wooden hulls, over two million fiberglass hulls, nearly two million aluminum hulls, and about another million boats made of plastic, ferrocement, steel fabric, and rubber.

Which brings us to why this book was written.

There is no one single source that I've been able to find which has focused on the care and maintenance of small boats.

There are excellent books available on the care and repair of wooden boats. If you have a fiberglass dinghy, there are still other books available. If you have a fabric folding boat or rubber life raft, there are good sources of information you could find. Ditto for engines and electronic gear. However, most books that attempt to cover many topics at once seem to get out of hand. Flip through them and you'll see what I mean. The illustrations will show a 42' ketch under sail or a twin-engine, three-deck steel yacht off some island in Greece. These make nice pictures and dress up a book, but only 3.6 percent of *all boats* in the U.S. are longer than 26 feet! In fact, 65 percent of all boats are under sixteen feet in length ("Class A"), and roughly 30 percent are in the 16' to 26' class.

This book was written for the small-boat owner and is a realistic approach to the care and maintenance of your boat and equipment. In it you will find very few "technical diagrams" of electrical wiring or complex cut-away views of engines and gear boxes. The text was prepared for a reader of average intelligence who can be expected to take on simple tasks with a minimum of tools. You will not become a master carpenter, mechanic, or electrical engineer, but you'll develop a confidence in your ability to maintain a safe and good-looking boat. And you'll have more fun.

Every major boating publication was reviewed for the most recent information on the subjects covered in these pages. Dozens of books were researched. Hundreds of letters were sent to manufacturers of boats and equipment. Interviews with experts were conducted.

In short, this book is one which I would have liked to find when I first went out on the water twenty years ago.

Good luck with it.

A fouled bottom can cut sailing speed, lead to even
more serious problems.

chapter 1

PAINTING, VARNISHING, FINISHING

How Important is Painting?

In putting together the many sections of this book, I often asked myself if I should attempt to develop an *order of priority* in the care and maintenance of boats. Was it more important to keep an eye out for wet rot, keep the engine tuned up, check out the RDF, or ensure that the running lights were operative? It immediately became apparent that priorities did not apply. Everything can become a matter of life and death; nothing can be overlooked. A frayed rope, weak batteries, or small patch of rot may seem relatively insignificant when you are tied to the dock, but can lead to serious consequences when out at sea.

But how important, then, can *painting* be when compared to the maintenance that directly involves the operation of a boat and the safety of its passengers?

Pretty important. And for a lot of reasons.

A beautifully turned-out boat is more than a matter of pride to its captain. A clean, well-cared-for boat with sparkling brightwork can be reason enough to open those paint cans every spring, but there are more fundamental elements involved in the task.

The lack of a bottom paint (or the use of an improper bottom paint) can lead to the growth of organisms on the bottom of the hull that will actually slow down the boat's forward speed and make it less responsive to the wheel or tiller. Not only can maneuverability be hindered to the point of danger, but some algae and sea grass growing from the bottom of your boat can actually foul your propeller and rudder system. Enough *filamentous bryozoa* dragging along behind you can cut your speed in half, and someday you'll find yourself unable to make headway against a four-knot tidal current.

Barnacles, annelids, and even mussels can find a home on the bottom of your boat if you don't take the proper measures. If you have a sailboat, your centerboard and centerboard trunk can become so fouled that you'll be unable to raise or lower the board—and, of course, if you can't lower your centerboard, you can only sail downwind. And at the end of the season, you'll discover that cleaning a filthy bottom is the dirtiest job there is.

The topsides are important, too. Flaking, chipping, peeling, and blistering paint will let moisture get behind the paint and rot a wooden boat, or rust a steel boat. Aluminum isn't safe, either. Salt spray and exposure to a sea air atmosphere can bring about corrosion on aluminum alloys. The white deposits you've seen on these hulls formed by the oxidation process are known as "white rust." Galvanic action will attack aluminum, and even the best alloys will gradually be eaten away. Fiberglass has good resistance to exposure, but the plastic resin coat will also gradually give way to the elements. Crazing and cracking can occur, as can discoloration and fading of color. Scuff marks, scratches, and dents get to look worse and worse. Any defects and imperfections that exist can become more serious.

In short, painting is very important.

Can you expect a film of chemical—thinner than the page of this book—to provide adequate protection? Yes. Today's paints are highly complex compounds and have never been better. If well applied, they will adhere to any surface and will "give" as your boat shrinks in the cold, expands in the heat, and twists on its axis while underway. They will withstand hurricanes, direct sunlight, scrapes, and the footsteps of you and your guests. No other film, not even steel or rubber, could begin to give you this service.

Plan Your Work

Because the cost of paint and materials you will use is very small compared to the effort you will put into the job, and because your goal is to protect and beautify an expensive piece of property, it is vital that you plan your work in advance. Decide how much of the work you can do in the yard and how much of it you should do after the boat is in the water. Can you work in the winter, under cover, to prepare the surfaces and get the interiors ready? Do you have all of the tools you will need?

If you want professional results, you will have to equip yourself with professional equipment. And you will have to take good care of it. Make a list of what you now have and what you will have to buy. Accumulate your gear far in advance and think out how you will proceed.

Key to easy painting maintenance is planning ahead, providing professional tools, and equipment.

Basic Tools

Paint brushes are the most important basic tools. Don't buy cheap synthetic brushes; they lose their bristles (usually while you're finishing up a very visible area) and do not flow the paint on freely. The "chopped-off" ends of the bristles are rough and don't provide a good final finish. Get brushes of pure natural bristle that taper slightly from the butt end to the tip. In better-grade brushes, the ends of the bristles are split into tiny forks or flags which will give you an even flow of paint. Make sure that the butt end is vulcanized in rubber.

Don't use the same brush for both paint and varnish; keep a separate set for each. Have one or two three-inch brushes for decks, topsides, and other large areas. A four-inch wall brush will be fine for the bottom. Some painters prefer an oval brush for this work, and I've been using an eleven-inch roller for some years with good results (and with no paint dripping down my arm). Small oval sash brushes, about one inch in width, are good for boottops and for work in close quarters. An excellent brush for varnish is the double-thick badger bristle with a full chisel point.

Nylon filament brushes are getting better and better and some painters prefer them. In theory, they improve with use. Try one or two and decide for yourself. I don't like them. The manufacturers of some of these will tell you that they can safely be used with products in which alcohol and lacquer solvents are used for thinning agents, but *there are paint products that should not be applied with Nylon brushes.*

Take care of your brushes; they can last you a lifetime. If you neglect them, you'll be buying a new set every spring. Never keep good brushes in water. This will destroy the natural spring of the bristle and the brush will be too soft to use. If you are storing a brush overnight, hang the brush in a keeping liquid of two parts raw linseed oil and one part turpentine, or in one of the many commercial brush-cleaning liquids on the market.

When you are using a brand-new brush, you should first remove any loose bristles (even the best brushes will have some) by first tapping the brush sharply against the palm of your hand and then twirling it between your hands. Next, soak the brush in a mixture of linseed oil and turpentine (half and half) for twenty-four hours.

When they are not in use, suspend the brushes with the ferrule just above the keeping liquid, and make sure the tips of the brushes are not touching the bottom. Drill a hole in the handle (if the brush did not come with one), and use a stiff wire to hold the brushes up. You can hang many brushes from one wire at the same time. When putting away a brush for a short time, I've driven a nail in the handle of the brush and suspended it from the edge of the paint can.

Before doing this, always wipe excess paint from

14

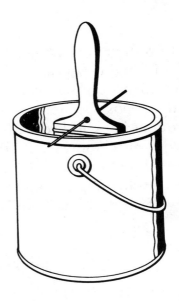

Best way to store brushes: suspend them in can as illustrated.

the brush against an old board or newspaper, and give the brush a cleaning with the thinner recommended by the paint manufacturer. Use turpentine and mineral spirits for cleaning oil paints and enamels. Use alcohol for shellac-type products.

If the brush is to be put away for a long time, give it a good cleaning in an appropriate thinner or solvent, and then wash it in warm soapy water. Work the soapy water between the bristles with your fingers. Use a steel comb to straighten out the bristles and get the curls and kinks out. Then put the brush away by wrapping it in kraft paper that has been soaked in raw linseed oil.

It may sound like a lot of work, but it takes only a few minutes and will save you, literally, hundreds of dollars in brushes in a lifetime.

If you don't follow the advice above, you'll walk

into your garage or cellar someday and find a bunch of stiff, paint-encrusted brushes that look as if they should be thrown away. Perhaps they should be, but it's possible to save them. Old brushes can be brought back to life with some of the newer paint-stripping chemicals on the market. You'll have to decide for yourself if the money should be spent on the cleaning products or on new brushes. I don't have that problem; I follow my own advice.

Spray Guns

Spray guns are great for large surfaces (and around the house for screens and wicker work). They are fast and do an even job once you've learned to use them. The time saved more than makes up for the time you'll spend masking the glass and brightwork you don't want sprayed. Remember, almost every manufacturer of paint will tell you that *you must never spray antifouling paint*! Some contain mercury and arsenic compounds and will clog either the gun or you.

There are two kinds of spray equipment: pressure and suction. Pressure guns are primarily for industrial work and heavy-duty yard work. For the incidental uses, suction guns are fine, less expensive, and easier to handle. The suction sprayer usually has a removable paint container connected to a gun that has a single air-pressure hose. The pressure

16

comes from a compressor and air tank. Suction guns are available in many sizes.

Spraying technique is a matter of practice, and your final result will depend on the type of paint you are using and the type of surface you are spraying it on. Work on the many ways of holding the gun, how close to the surface to keep the nozzle, how fast to move the gun, and how much thinner to add. For spraying, brush-consistency paint is usually thinned with one pint of commercial thinner to every gallon of paint. Test the spray on an old board before starting on your boat, and adjust the spray nozzle to suit. Keep your equipment clean and in good repair. After spraying, clean out the container and put in thinner. Flush this through the

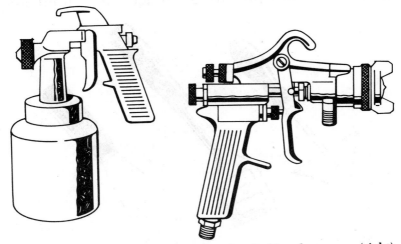

Two types of spray guns: suction (left) and pressure (right).

system; then disassemble the nozzle and other parts, cleaning everything in thinner. Let all parts dry before reassembling the gun.

Scrapers

The saw steel scraper your great-grandfather left you is still the best kind to use on your boat. Not only can it be used for seam cleaning, but it will also remove all flakes, chips, and blisters. These scrapers are hard steel and triangular in shape, and can handle almost any job. Other shapes can be used, but make sure you don't buy the 88-cent specials from Japan that will lose their edge before you get started. Putty knives are also useful to move away loose paint and prepare a surface. Be careful not

Keep scrapers sharp; round off corners to prevent gouging out wood.

to dig in scars into the wood with the edges of these tools. Hook scrapers are excellent for removing old paint that has been softened with the new chemical paint removers. Keep your scrapers sharpened with a fine-toothed flat file, and keep the cutting edge at the same angle it was when you bought it. Round off the corners to help prevent digging into the wood.

To clean out seams you can easily make another kind of scraper from the tang of an old file. Simply heat it red-hot and bend the sharp end to a ninety-degree angle so that you can get into a seam and remove loose putty and caulking. File the tang to a sharp point to get a clean bite into the wood. Then reheat it until it's again red-hot, and plunge it into ice-cold water. This will give the steel a good temper and reharden it.

Wire brushes are also good scrapers and can be used for removing loose paint and rust from metal surfaces. There are block types and narrow ones with handles; ask your paint dealer to recommend the proper one for the job, or get one of each and use your judgment.

Sandpapers

Sandpaper isn't the most accurate term to use any-more, because sand is not always the abrasive used. Your choice of papers is very wide, but for preparing the surface of your boat you'll need only a few types. Garnet papers and aluminum oxide papers are adequate, especially the open coats which come in sheets measuring nine by eleven inches. Non-fill silicone carbide papers will not clog as fast as other types and are also good for boat maintenance. Unless you have special problems, three grades are all that you'll need: Number one (50) is your coarsest grade, for the heavy work; 1/0 (80) will serve for the medium grade to start getting your surface in shape; 3/0 (120) is for fine finishing and a smooth surface.

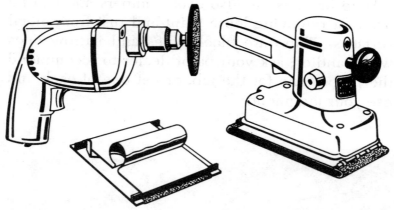

Power sanders and sanding block.

That's really all you need for a good paint job, but if you want a mirror-like surface, go to 5/0 (180) or 6/0 (220). These are especially good for rubbing down between coats of varnish work or for the final finishing of racing bottoms.

Sandpaper doesn't wear out as fast as you think. Use a soft brush to clean out clogged paper. When

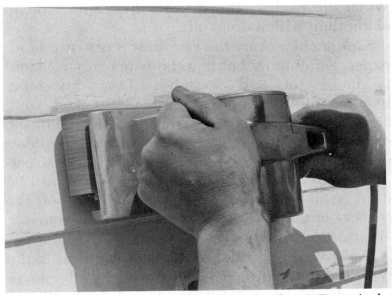

Power sander is great for large areas (above). Two mistakes (below): don't sand without gloves, don't sand without block of some kind.

paper gets worn, begin using it as the next finer grade. Experienced painters will rub two pieces of sandpaper together in order to remove oversized particles that might dig into the work and leave marks. "Wet" papers are used to give an unusually high gloss to finishes. Soak them in water before using and keep them wet while working with them. When done, clean the surfaces first with a damp cloth, then with a dry cloth.

Sanding blocks are the very best way to use sand-paper. Sanding by holding the paper in your hand is inefficient and wasteful. Tear the nine-by-eleven-inch sheets in four pieces and wrap around the sanding block. Use a commercial block, or make your own by facing it with sponge rubber or two layers from an old inner tube. Felt, old carpeting, or any material with some "give" can also be used against the back of the paper. Round off the corners of the block to make it easier on yourself. Wear cotton work gloves.

Never use steel wool on a boat, regardless of the type of material from which it is made. Little pieces of steel are always left behind, and they will rust in the damp atmosphere near boats. It's impossible to get all the steel shards off by wiping with a cloth, and your boat will look progressively worse as the season wears on until it takes on an evenly distributed rust color. Unless you've decided to paint your boat a rust color, use bronze wool available at your marine store.

Putty Knives and Caulking

Putty knives can be put to many uses on a boat. Old paint can be removed; small cracks can be filled in. These knives can be used to fill in seams when you are caulking, and they'll open a can of beer in an emergency. Get a good one with a tapered, flexible blade. Keep it clean; don't let paint build up on it.

Putty knives alone can't do the complete caulking job. You'll need a caulking iron to lay in the cotton "rope" and some advice on how to use it. Practice is the best way, after watching someone else do it. A broad knife will be needed to work in your compound. A caulking gun can be used, either the hand-operated or the pressure type. All boats have need for occasional caulking: wooden boats definitely do, and even fiberglass boats may need "water-proofing" where the deck piece meets the hull and around all wooden coaming.

Removing Old Paint

A blowtorch is an outstanding tool for removing old paint, but it is dangerous. Burning and charring the wood or fiberglass beneath the paint can prove to be a costly mistake. Leaving the torch too near a fuel tank will cause an embarrassing explosion. There are many types of blowtorches you can buy or rent, and a little practice on an old board will soon make you proficient. Just remember never to set it down pointed at something you'd like to keep, and always have a fire extinguisher handy.

An infrared lamp, the kind you use on your aching back, will also remove paint if you hold it about an inch to an inch and one-half from the work. Move the lamp along slowly and peel off the paint with a broad knife as it blisters. An old flatiron sitting on a paint film will soften it enough for you to lift it off. This is especially good when working with canvas-covered decks or canoes.

Power sanding, when there is electrical power available, will save you much time and give you professional results. It isn't necessary to buy the equipment you need; most of the tools can be rented. The rotary sanding discs that fit at the end of your power drill can be used, but you have to be careful

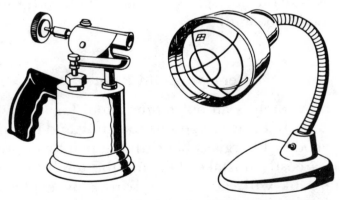

Blow torch (left) is best way to remove old paint, but safety precautions must be exercised. Infrared lamp can also be used.

not to leave behind deep swirls when the disc bites into the wood. Vibrating or belt sanders are better and easier to use, but with a little practice the disc sander will serve for most jobs. Open-coat production sandpaper only should be used, and don't use power sanders *between* coats.

What you wear while preparing a surface and painting it is important. Wear old clothes, of course, but make it the kind of protective clothing that will not let the paint get to your skin. You may have a serious allergy to some of the chemical formulations and experience a bad reaction. Wear gloves, especially when you are painting overhead. When sanding, a gauze mask over your mouth and nose is advisable. Lead, zinc, arsenic, mercury, and other ingredients in paints can make you very ill.

The final thing you'll want to do before actually applying the paint is to go over the surface with a tack rag. Don't ignore this step. A good tack rag will remove the last trace of sanding dust, grime, and other debris that would prevent perfect adhesion of the paint. You can buy tack rags, but you're better off making your own. Start with a large piece of cloth that is lint-free and dip it in hot water. Wring it out and sprinkle turpentine over it. Wring it out again and sprinkle varnish on it. Then wring it out a third time, and work it between your hands to distribute the liquids you have added. Now it is ready for use. Keep in a tightly covered jar between paintings and it will last a long time.

When and Where to Paint

Paint your boat in a hermetically sealed building where you can control the temperature and humidity. Failing that, you'll probably paint your boat like everyone else: outdoors in the boatyard, where wind and passing cars will raise dust that will settle on your fresh paint job. It'll start to rain; then the temperature will drop and the varnish won't set up right.

If you want a first-class job that will last, select your painting days carefully. Wait a day or two, or a weekend or two, for the right conditions. You can do a lot of work indoors on any parts of the boat that can be removed and brought into a garage or a shed. If the weather is dry and warm but windy, paint the interiors.

High humidity can ruin your paint job. Fog is visible humidity. Don't paint in the very early morning until after the dew has burned away. Don't paint in hot midday sun; the paint will dry too fast and "lap" or wrinkle (the surface will dry long before the paint below the surface; when it shrinks and cures, the top surface will pucker). Don't paint too far into the evening. Give the paint some time to start drying before the moist evening air moves in.

The Paint

Try to stay with the same kind of paint once you've found something you can work with easily and that gives you the kind of results you want. Some paints don't work well when applied on top of other paints. Never put a hard paint over a soft paint. Under no circumstances should you apply paints containing active solvents over the more ordinary oxidizing paints. Enamels don't work over paints with a linseed oil base. Lacquers, two-part epoxies, and vinyl paints will tend to soften the conventional paints over which they are applied. Try to remember what you used last; look for the old can in the basement or locker, and check with your paint dealer. If you're unsure, test a small area.

Most painting results that are less than satisfactory arise from the use of improperly mixed paint. If the front of your boat (usually the pointy part) winds up a different color from the afterdeck or if the deck wrinkles and the side of the boat hull has "curtains," chances are you didn't mix the paint properly.

Pour off one-third or so from one can into another and stir what remains until it is of a smooth consistency, with no lumps or thick goo in the bottom of the can. Keep stirring as you return the paint you transferred to the other can. Then pour the paint back and forth many times and stir frequently. When you buy your paint, ask the dealer to put it in his agitator for you. But check it out when you get home, anyway. Do *not* agitate or shake varnish. If you do, little bubbles will form and you won't be able to brush them out. A pock-marked surface will result.

Strain your paint. Cheesecloth or a fine screen

will not only remove stray debris, but will also improve the consistency of your paint. Pour two or three inches of the paint into the container you will be working with. Don't put too much paint in the can or bucket, or it will creep up the bristles to the heel of the brush and overload it. Remove excess paint from your brush by tapping it against the inside of the container, or drawing against a wire affixed diagonally across the top. Wiping the brush on the side of the can will only cause drips. Never draw your brush sideways against anything.

Some people have written about how to hold a paintbrush: they've described the pistol grip, the pen grip, and other artful ways to greet a paintbrush. Hold the brush the way you want to, and if your hand gets tired, take a break.

Painting Wooden Hulls

Wood is, of course, the traditional substance for boatbuilding, but it is fast giving way to fiberglass and other materials. Painting a new wooden boat is not much trouble, but going over an older boat can take a few days. We've discussed the preparation of surfaces, but if you're faced with many thicknesses of paint in bad condition, you should get it all off down to the wood, either with a blowtorch or with the new chemical paint strippers/removers. Some of these solvents leave a waxy residue that will have to be removed; others leave a residue that can be washed off with water. In either case, follow up by sanding. If the paint is in good shape, simply sand enough to provide good adhesion.

If you are working on a planked boat, as opposed to one of plywood construction, clean out the seams if they need it. There are primers you should use in the seams before caulking to maximize adhesion of the compound. Check the can.

Nicks, dents, gouges, tool marks, scrapes, exposed screw heads, and other imperfections can be covered with trowel cements and surfacing compounds. Sand smooth again before painting. The first step in painting over any bare wood surface, whether it is the entire hull or merely a small patch that

**Caulking seamed boat
before repainting.**

you worked over, is to apply a coat of sealer. Let this dry completely, and then sand off any wood fibers that have risen above the surface. Some open-grained wood, such as mahogany, will need a wood filler before painting.

Glazing the surface of bare wood is a step that many painters often forget, but it is essential for a smooth finish. Trowel cement can be applied with a broad putty knife to fill in any remaining imperfections and open pores. Thinned out, it can be applied with a brush. I've even done it with an old rag, spreading it around and working it in as if it were a stain. The surface should be ready in four hours or so for sanding and, subsequently, for the undercoat.

After the undercoat has dried and been sanded smooth, check for any final dents and scratches and fill these in with a good surfacing compound. The second undercoat is sometimes mixed with some of the final finish coat. You can test this for yourself. Remember that undercoats and primers come in colors. If you intend to paint your final finish in blue or another dark color, don't use an undercoat that is white or "neutral," as it will show through whenever you dent or scratch the boat.

From here on, it's a case of waiting for a nice day and painting your final coats—preferably with a new brush—and sanding. One coat will usually do for most boats. I use two and find it's worth the extra time and effort.

Painting Fiberglass Hulls

The shiny, faultless surface of fiberglass will not last forever. It will dull with the action of wind, water, sun, and temperature changes. Repairs of the outer surface will mar the finish and require painting. After three years of having a red hull, your wife will want a French blue hull with a heliotrope boottop. Sooner or later, you'll be painting your fiberglass boat.

Fiberglass boats are generally made of reinforced polyester in metal female molds. The smooth outer surface between the polyester and the mold is known as the "gel coat" and is made of polyester resins and various chemical agents. A mold release either is applied directly to the metal mold or is mixed in with the gel coat. Because mold-release ingredients are formulated to prevent adhesion to the metal mold, they will also act to prevent adhesion to other things, such as paint. This is why the painting of a fiberglass boat requires special instructions and preparation.

Not all paints will give the same results, and it is best to use the type recommended by the boat manufacturer and not what you happen to have on hand or what the paint dealer had on special last week. Generally, paints incorporating polyurethane resins will be satisfactory—if the surface has been properly prepared.

The gloss on a fiberglass surface must be removed

if the paint is to adhere to it. The grit of sandpaper will leave tiny grooves on the surface and provide a "key" for the paint to hold on to. Sand *until no gloss remains* and you have a dull mat finish.

Sanding may have removed all of the wax and mold-release agents from the surface, but don't count on it. There are many commercial "de-waxers" and solvent washes available, and you should use one of them. Don't use a fast-evaporating solvent such as acetone or tuluol or you will simply be moving the wax around and redepositing it someplace else on the hull. Use plenty of old rags and use the proper solvent liberally; then follow up by wiping with clean, dry rags.

You may find after doing this that you have "revived" some of the gloss to the surface. Actually, you have removed the sanding dust you created, which gave you the appearance of a mat finish. If any glossy areas remain, you must sand these again. Then clean the dust off again.

There are paints for fiberglass that do not require a primer and whose final finish will be superior in gloss and color retention to the original gel coat. Undercoats and primers are necessary only if the surface is in bad shape. Chips, deep scratches, and the like should be gone over with one of the surfacing compounds and trowel cements made for use on fiberglass. A coat of paint over the repair followed by sanding is then recommended.

Painting Aluminum Hulls

Salt spray is the worst thing for aluminum, but the alloy can be attacked by other things as well. The chemicals that now pollute our waters can also cause harm, as can the galvanic action set up when there are other metals in the boat. Larger boats with electrical equipment aboard are more susceptible to this.

When aluminum boats are being made, there is a thin film of oil or lubricant on the sheet metal to facilitate the handling of parts and for protection. An abrasive cleaner or commercial grease cutter will remove this. Because the metal is smooth like fiberglass, it should be lightly sanded to provide a rough surface to which the paint can adhere. If sandblasting equipment is available, use 80-mesh white silica sand.

Bare-metal prime coats will provide a mild "etching" to the metal and offer better adhesion. To counter pitting and corrosion, particularly at welded joints, a barrier coat of paint (*not* one containing red lead) should be applied. Some manufacturers also recommend a coat of antigalvanic paint followed by a second barrier coat, followed by another coat of antigalvanic paint and a third barrier coat.

The painting of aluminum boats can become very complex, but it need not be. Because of the special problems presented by this alloy, there are many "systems" that can be followed. The best advice is to select the products from a reputable paint manufacturer and decide which "system" is suitable to your situation. Your dealer and the instructions on the paint can will be your best guides.

Painting Steel Hulls and Surfaces

Most small boats are not made of steel, but much of the equipment aboard is: centerboards, engines, keels, various fittings, etc. Like aluminum, steel is subject to galvanic corrosion; unlike aluminum, it can also rust. Rust will cause anything made of steel to lose its pleasant appearance, will stain other materials around it, and will cause the metal to lose its strength.

All grease, oil, and other contaminants must be eliminated before a steel surface is painted. Rust and scales must be removed entirely. Sandblasting or wire brushing (with power if you have it) are recommended. In addition, there are solvents you can use which will result in a clean surface ready for painting.

Barrier coats, such as red lead primers, are extremely important here. They provide protection against electrolytic attack. As with aluminum, a metal painting "system" consisting of various types of paint coatings is used in order to give maximum protection. Bare-metal prime coat, followed by one or two coats of barrier paint, should go on before the final coat. Stay with the system offered by one manufacturer so that all paints will be compatible.

Bottom Painting

Bottom paints must do more work than any other kind of paint. Which kind you select and how you apply it are more important than any other painting project you will undertake on your boat. Not only must bottom paints provide protection against the elements, but they must also minimize fouling by organisms in the water.

The kind of bottom paint you select should be decided by the locality where you have your boat. Ordinarily your dealer knows this and stocks the kind suitable for your climate. It will be to your advantage to obtain the best available bottom paint, because if you don't you'll be paying for hauling your boat out and doing it over again.

Bottom paints contain toxicants—such as cuprous oxide, metallic flake copper, and mercury or organo-tin compounds—that kill or prevent the growth of water-borne organisms. There is also a binder that will ensure that this toxicant is at the surface ready to do its job by the process of leaching, exfoliation, or "migration."

Bottom paints will fail when unpredictable things happen in the water where you keep your boat:

storms, weather changes, an increase in the salinity of the water, pollution. These may combine to cause a sudden infestation of marine organisms that will be attracted to your hull faster than the toxicants in your bottom paint can fight them off.

If the bottom was not properly prepared, the bottom paint will not adhere and do its work. If you run aground, or hit an obstruction underwater, the bottom paint could be scraped off. Metal bottoms may blister if the barrier coat was insufficient. Zinc anodes may set up a reaction that will make your paint ineffective. Not mixing the paint will leave the poison in the bottom of the can. Adding too much thinner to stretch your paint will give you inadequate deposits of poison.

When painting bare wooden hulls, use no primers or preservatives or undercoatings of any kind. Work the paint right into the wood and you will get maximum protection. In areas where teredos are a problem, your first coat should be of an organotin antifoulant. This will seep into the wood and give you protection if the outer coat of bottom paint is ever scraped away. Two or three coats are better than one.

It isn't necessary to clean an old bottom down to bare wood. Simply scrape or sand away any chipping or peeling areas until you have a clean surface to which new paint will adhere.

Fiberglass bottoms are as likely to foul as wooden

bottoms and also need good bottom paints. A primer is ordinarily needed, and a clean, well-prepared surface is important. Procedure will vary depending on the type of paint you employ.

Aluminum also fouls, and, in addition to the antifouling paint, requires a barrier coat (or two or three). Do *not* use red lead paint, as it will embrittle the aluminum. Do *not* use mercury compounds. If the bottom paint you use contains copper, use it only if a thick barrier coat is first laid on. The best paints to use are those with organotin compounds. These will not have any chemical effect upon the aluminum. The use of a painting "system," as referred to earlier, will depend on the type of paint you eventually elect to buy.

Steel surfaces below the water need first a primer and then a barrier coat of red lead before the two final coats of antifouling paint are applied.

Antifouling paint is not essential if your boat is a day sailer that spends most of its time on the beach or on a trailer. If you "dry sail," you are better off with a hard racing bottom.

Unless bottom is cleaned well, paint will not adhere.

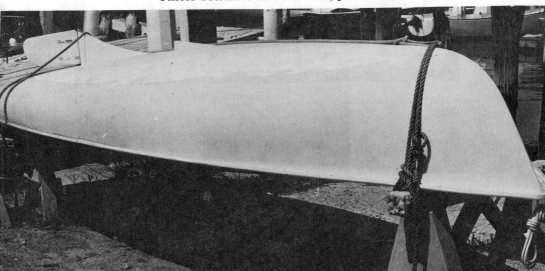

Use marine grade paints for interiors.

Cabins and Interiors

This is a matter of personal preference. Select a high gloss, semigloss, or flat finish to reflect as much light as you feel is comfortable for you. Don't make the mistake of using ordinary household paints simply because the interiors are not exposed to the outside elements. Use good marine-grade paints and prepare the surfaces just as carefully as you do on the deck and exterior hull. Light colors will give you an airy feeling of "extra" space below. Naturally finished wood is also very pleasing and will give a fine furniture-like appearance to your interiors.

Mildew is a problem in any enclosed space, and getting ventilation below to forestall it is always difficult. Mildew will ruin your work if it gets a foothold. It is a mold that spawns with increasing rapidity once it gets started. Kill it with one of the commercial cleaners for this purpose, or use trisodium or sodium hypochlorite mixed in water.

Paint overhead first and work down. For hard-to-get-at places, use one or two aerosol paint cans (compatible with the paint that you brushed on.)

Varnishing

Wood brightwork on a boat is very pleasing to the eye, and imparts an aesthetic balance to break up the large painted areas. Its condition also tells a great deal about the owner.

For non-skid surfaces, paint with "sand" paint.

40

If you are about to varnish new wood, you must first build up a foundation on which to apply varnish. First, the bare wood should be sanded until it is smooth. Don't use too fine a sandpaper, as this will simply polish the surface and not provide a good "tooth" to the wood.

A wood filler is needed on open-grained wood. The paste should be thinned until creamy and applied with a coarse cloth, rubbing across the grain. When it is dry, go over it lightly with sandpaper. Tightly-grained wood such as fir, juniper, pine, etc., does not require wood filler, but all bare plywood should be so treated. Plywood should also get a priming or sealing coat before it receives varnish. Plywood looks much better under varnish if you have first stained it.

If you are varnishing over old varnish, simply sand sufficiently to provide good adhesion. However, if the old surface is stained or discolored with dark patches, you should get down to bare wood and bleach. Use a strong solution of oxalic acid, made by dissolving crystals in warm water, adding crystals until they no longer dissolve. Work in the sunlight and paint on the solution until the dark spots disappear; then go over all of your wood until you get an even-colored appearance. Follow up with a solution of borax mixed in hot water. This will neutralize the bleaching effect. Let the surface dry for at least twelve hours before sanding.

Wood that has been stripped of old varnish should also get a treatment of wood filler.

Sanding should always be done in the direction of the grain, and between each coat. Never varnish unless the temperature is between 60 and 85 degrees Fahrenheit. Never shake or agitate varnish. Never wipe your brush on the edge of the can, as this will create a froth of bubbles to fall into your can. Bubbles in the varnish cannot be completely brushed out. Use a good varnish brush that has never been used for paint. Use a full brush and apply a generous coat; do not overbrush or try to get too thin a coat. Many manufacturers recommend three or four coats over bare wood, and one or two over old surfaces in good condition. I use seven coats until the surface looks like a wet crystal ball, and can sometimes go two years before having to varnish again. Use your tack rag after sanding between coats.

Wood filler is essential for open-grained wood and after stripping off old varnish.

Teak Finishing

Never seal or varnish teak. It is meant to be a "minimum maintenance" wood whose beauty will be lost if conventional coatings are applied. There are commercial teak cleaners on the market that will remove oil, food, and soil stains and will not bleach the wood. Some contain phosphoric acid, and you should be careful to keep the solution away from your eyes and out of the reach of children. There are also special "sealers" and shields for teak which will help preserve it and protect it from stains. Some contain a fungicide to prevent or inhibit bacterial or fungal stains.

Non-Skid Surfaces

Decks don't provide the surest footing when dry, and can be murder when slick with water. Old-timers used canvas for decking material, because it has a woven textured surface and makes possible better friction between the deck and your foot. Very few boats have canvas decks today, but non-skid surfaces can be applied in a number of ways.

Some paints can be purchased with little granules of "sand" or grit in collodial suspension. These will give a sandpaper finish to the topcoat and provide good traction. You can also buy these granules separately and add them to whatever paint you are using. You can use fine beach sand in your paint, or sprinkle it on carefully after you have applied the paint. Adhesive-backed rubber or vinyl strips can also be laid down wherever there is heavy traffic and hence the need for extra safety.

Bilges

All boats have bilges. They get filthy with oil, gas, cigarette butts, leaves, and general corruption. They smell. If you allow the sludge to build up and do nothing about it until after the season is over, you'll have a tough job on your hands cleaning it up.

During the season, while your boat is in the water, pour a good bilge cleaner below that will dissolve the gunk and slosh it around during the normal operation of the boat. Then pump it out. Repeat as needed.

Dirt alone will not harm your bilges, but a neglected bilge will soon show signs of rot on a wooden boat. Some boatmen prefer not to paint the inside of a hull below the water line: they argue that the wood must "breathe." Others slap on paint ten layers thick. The best thing you can do is to apply one or two coats of preservative at the start of every season, and, if appearance is a factor to you, paint over it once after the preservative has dried. Rot is a fungus and needs to be killed. The commercial preservatives will contain copper salts of napthenic acid or pentachlorophenol. You may use a spray gun to get at hard-to-reach corners, but follow the manufacturer's directions on the can: some bilge paints should *not* be sprayed.

Best way to maintain bilges is to apply preservative at the start of every season.

The Engine and Metal Fittings

Keep the engine painted or it will rust. Degrease it, use an appropriate primer for the metal, and finish with a rust-inhibiting topcoat. Use an aerosol can and make the job easier on yourself. Follow the steps previously noted for painting metals for proper surface preparation. Stanchions, davits, tanks, and other metal fittings, unless chromed or of some alloy that does not require protection, should also be painted regularly as needed.

A clean engine is much less likely to break down.

Painting the Trailer

See Chapter Nine for detailed tips on the maintenance of trailers (and cartoppers). Painting is only part of the maintenance work required, because trailers, including the axle, wheels, and bearings, are often completely immersed in water. For strength, they are usually made of metal, and that can rust. Follow the tips on painting steel noted above. If rust spots show through the paint after a season, chances are you don't have a good primer against the metal. If water and oxygen get beneath the paint, rust will form and corrode your trailer.

How Much Paint to Buy

Nothing is more annoying than getting into the painting of your boat and running out of paint at noon on Sunday with all the stores closed. Experience will be your best guide, but it's still possible to guess wrong. Painting over bare wood will require almost twice as much paint as going over an old surface. Use Table 1 as a general guide only. If you overbuy, you can still use the leftover paint for touch ups, or save it until next season. If your paint dealer is friendly enough, he'll let you take what you think you need and return the excess for credit if the cans are unopened.

Table 1
Estimates of Average Paint Requirements

For Two Coats Over Existing Finish (Over bare wood, quantities will be about double those shown. Less will be required on fiberglass or metal.)

SIZE	TOPSIDE	BOTTOM	BOOTTOP	DECK	VARNISH	FLYBRIDGE	INTERIOR	ENGINE
10' Dinghy	1 qt.	1 pt.	—	—	1 qt.	—	—	—
14' Rowboat	2 qts.	1 qt.	—	—	—	—	—	—
14' Outboard	1 qt.	1 qt.	½ pt.	1 pt.	1 qt.	—	—	single aerosol
18' Runabout	1 qt.	3 qts.	½ pt.	1 qt.	1 qt.	—	—	single aerosol
20' Sailboat	2 qts.	3 qts.	½ pt.	3 qts.	2 qts.	—	—	—
24' Runabout	2 qts.	3 qts.	½ pt.	1½ qts.	2 qts.	—	—	single aerosol
24' Utility	2 qts.	3 qts.	½ pt.	1½ qts.	1 qt.	—	—	single aerosol
25' Cruiser	3 qts.	3 qts.	1 pt.	2 qts.	2 qts.	—	2 qts.	single aerosol

Note: Reprinted by permission of the publisher from
How to Paint Your Boat
(Woolsey Marine Industries, Inc., 1970).

A Checklist of Do's and Don't's

• Read the directions on the can. Most painting failures are directly attributable to painters who "knew how to paint" but didn't familiarize themselves with the products they were using.

• Make sure the paint you buy is appropriate for your boat and compatible with the paint over which you will be applying it.

• Stir paints thoroughly—particularly bottom paints. Keep them stirred. Strain the paint until it is clean and consistent in viscosity.

• Never shake or stir varnish. Bubbles will remain and ruin your surface.

• Thin carefully. Most paints come ready to use and do not require thinning. If thinning is necessary, thin only enough to make the paint workable. Too much thinner will completely alter the chemical composition of the paint and ruin it. Even for spray guns, the addition of 10 percent thinner should be more than enough. Use only the thinners recommended by the manufacturer.

• Do not paint on cold or wet days, over dewy surfaces, in the late evening, in direct sunlight, or on windy days when dust can settle on your work.

• Make sure the surfaces are clean and dry—free of grease, oil, dirt, and sanding dust.

• Sand old paint and varnish to remove chalk and gloss.

• *Spread* paint and enamels. *Flow on* varnish.

• Allow enough time between coats. If you can dig your fingernail in the paint, wait a little longer before putting on the next coat.

• Don't mix paints from two different manufacturers.

• Don't apply antifouling paints containing mercury with a spray gun.

• If you use a paint remover, go over the area with alcohol or turpentine to clean away any residue.

Identifying Paint Failures

Blistering means that moisture has found its way beneath the paint, or that moisture was there and you painted over it. This happens on wood, fiberglass, aluminum, and steel. On wooden boats, scrape to bare wood and let it dry out. Use a heat lamp, but don't get too close.

Peeling occurs when the paint actually splits and begins to fall away. Sometimes the fault is with the paint, but usually the reason is that the surface over which it was applied was too smooth and did not offer a good grip. Re-do.

Flaking occurs when very old paint simply breaks

down and loses its composition. Unlike blistering and peeling, which are the result of conditions under the paint, flaking paint is paint that has become brittle and is falling away. The best remedy is to go down to the bare surface and start from scratch.

Alligatoring is a pattern of large, deep cracks. It is often caused by improper undercoating with

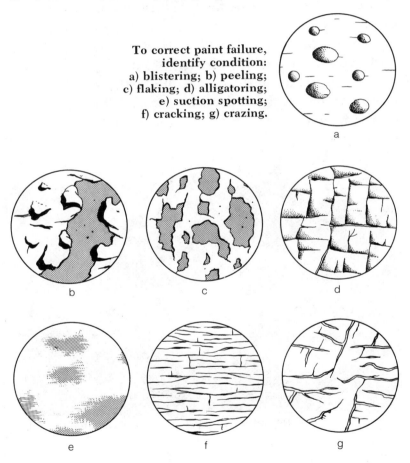

To correct paint failure, identify condition: a) blistering; b) peeling; c) flaking; d) alligatoring; e) suction spotting; f) cracking; g) crazing.

primer or sealer, or by painting over undercoats that have not thoroughly dried.

Suction spotting is noticed when some areas soak in more paint than others and an uneven appearance results. This is due to poor priming and sealing.

Cracking and crazing can be caused by age, as with flaking, but very often are the result of movement of the painted surface. Whether a boat is made of wood or steel, it will twist and bend when in use. Temperature changes will also make it shrink and expand. A better grade of paint may solve this.

Washing is a condition in which the top layer of paint can be washed or wiped away. This is caused by painting on a damp day or when the temperature is too low.

Peeling usually occurs when surface is too smooth.

What Color to Paint Your Boat

Paint it any color you want— it's your boat. But remember a few simple tips. Dark hulls will make a boat look high out of the water and bulky. White and light-colored hulls usually make a boat look long and sleek.

Don't paint the hull a light color and everything topside a dark color. Your boat will look as if it's about to turn over. Two colors are enough for any boat unless you're going to a Turkish wedding.

Dark colors absorb more heat. Light colors will reflect ultraviolet rays and keep the boat cooler. Bottom paints are only seen by fish unless you are heeling over or capsized. Select a color you think the fish will like. Boottops should be of a complementary color. A blue hull with a green bottom does not call for a purple boottop stripe.

The interiors should harmonize with outside colors. Don't get into an entirely different paint scheme, regardless of what your wife says. Let her exercise her color sense on the cushions and curtains.

If you're in doubt, go to a marina and look at color combinations on other boats.

Specialty Products

In addition to paint, many other preparations and finishes now available can make getting your boat ready easier than ever.

Cleaners and solvents are made for every imaginable use: for cleaning wood, fiberglass, metals, ferrocement, vinyl seats and decks, motors, windshields, bilges, and chemical toilets.

Trowel cements, surfacing compounds, seam compounds, caulking and sealants, bedding compounds, wood fillers, vinyl and "plastic" paint systems, two-part epoxy paints, mastics, "tie-coats" to bond together two other paints—these are just a few of the materials that will give your boat a beautiful finish. There is, in fact, no excuse for you not to turn out a professional paint job.

Protecting Your Paint Job

There's no point in doing all that work if it is to be ruined through neglect. Your investment in time and money should be looked after.

Keep your boat clean. Right after pulling in at the dock, hose the boat down with fresh water and get the salt off. Keep the boat free of dust, soot, and air-borne pollution. Occasionally use a good boat soap and a sponge mop to wash down the topsides. Use an abrasive cleaner for tough stains.

Don't wear hard-soled footgear aboard and ask your guests not to. Don't let sand and dirt stay on your painted surfaces; wash them off. Wipe up any spills of oil or fuel immediately.

Unpainted fiberglass surfaces should be kept

clean with products especially formulated for this purpose. They should then be waxed with marine paste wax to help protect the gel coat.

Summary

With the information in this chapter and the directions on the actual products you will buy, you should be able to come out with a painless and professional job. If you have any questions, ask your dealer or write to the manufacturer direct.

chapter 2

THE FIBERGLASS HULL

Fiberglass is stronger than any other boat material except steel. It takes abuse better than any other material; it requires maintenance less often; and it is simple to repair when damaged.

Although this material can resist the kind of damage that would be more visible on boats made of wood or aluminum, it too can become scratched, dented, gouged, and even stove in through the hull.

Minor Repairs

Minor repairs are just that: minor. They can be effected in a matter of minutes. Small scratches can be buffed away and the boat rewaxed with one of the many commercial preparations on the market. Dents and gouges can be filled in very easily by following these simple steps. First, clean the area thoroughly. A scouring cleanser will serve, and you can use a solvent sold for the purpose (see Chapter One). Next, roughen up the area with sandpaper to provide a "tooth" for adhesion of the compound you will be using to fill in the space. You can enlarge the damaged area and feather the edges if you wish. Wipe the sanding dust away.

Mix the resin and hardener to the manufacturer's instructions. (These will vary, depending on what type of fiberglass filler you decide to buy.) With a clean mixing stick or putty knife, work the mixture into the hole you are filling, making sure you have good contact everywhere. Apply more mixture than you actually need to fill the hole, topping it with an extra $1/16$ of an inch and overlapping onto the feathered edges. This should cure overnight and be ready for sanding the following morning. Finish off with a fine sandpaper and follow up with a rubbing compound to get a high gloss finish. If your mixture had a coloring agent in it, you are ready to wax over it and the job is done. If you are going to paint over your work, do not wax.

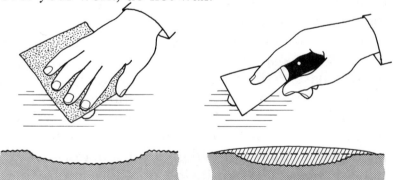

Fiberglass repair: a) sand, top left; b) fill in gouged out area, top right; sand down to hull line, bottom right.

Major Repairs

Fiberglass can crack and break if hit hard enough, and a hole can be punched through the hull. This can be repaired with one of the "repair kits" at your dealer's (more than one if the damage is extensive), or you can buy epoxy resins, hardeners, glass cloth, mats, and other materials you'll need individually to suit the job at hand.

Inside Patches

Repairs are done systematically, step by step, and can be handled very easily. First, the damaged area is cut away with a saw. Go beyond the damage slightly, until you are sure that you have reached the unfractured material. Next, with a file or sander, bevel an edge to the hole you have made. This will give a grip to the patch you will install later. Then, depending on the size of the hole, sand around it for two to four inches on the outside of the hull. Only by sanding can you be sure to remove all of the mold-release agent; sanding will also give a better purchase to the resin you will be applying. Now you must sand on the *inside* of the hull for a distance of at least six inches. This is because you will be patching from the inside of the boat, which is the preferred method and will give you a better-looking outside surface. (If an inside repair is impossible, you can make a good outside patch by following the directions in the next section.)

When sanding on the inside, feather toward the edges slightly but not so much as to lose the outside beveled edge made earlier. Clean off the sanding dust.

Now cut a piece of acetate (from an art supply or hardware store) three or four inches larger than the hole, and give it a coat of paste wax. If you have no acetate, you can use a piece of cardboard covered with cellophane or plastic wrap. You are ready to cut out a patch of fiberglass cloth or mat. This should be two or three inches bigger than the hole. Whether you use a fiberglass cloth or a thicker mat will depend on the thickness of the hull you are working with. Measure this before going to your dealer. You can use cloth in layers to build up the patch, but you will not be able to work as fast. Remember, the resin and hardener combination will set up very fast, depending on your mix and the temperature.

Lay the patch on your acetate or cellophane-covered cardboard and saturate it with your resin mix. Now set the patch over the hole, and, using masking tape, make the acetate or cardboard conform to the outside shape of the hull. Use plenty of tape and make sure the platch is flat, tight, and "fair" with the hull and follows the natural lines of tape and make sure the patch is flat, tight, and

Working now on the inside of the hull, begin to lay up layers of cloth against the patch that shows through the hole, overlapping the hole by six inches all around. Criss-cross the layers so that the weave of each layer of cloth is in a different direction from the previous layer. You should cut these layers out in advance, before mixing the resin and hardener. Apply plenty of resin to the cloth between layers and make sure the cloth is completely saturated. As you work, remove all bubbles in the resin and cloth; these are weak spots. The number of layers you apply will depend on the thickness of your hull. Your repair should be at least as thick as the hull. This may require six to ten layers.

Once the patch has cured, you may remove the acetate sheet you used to keep the patch against the hull. You may want to "post-cure" your work with a heat lamp for an hour or two. This is not essential, but if you do it, be sure that the lamp never gets closer than eight inches to your work. Use nothing stronger than a 300-watt bulb.

Now you can sand the outside of the hull smooth and fair. Cover with an epoxy finish coat the color of the boat and follow painting instructions in the first chapter.

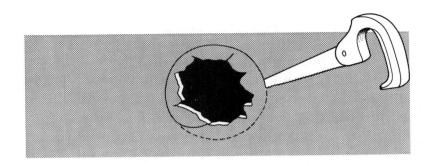

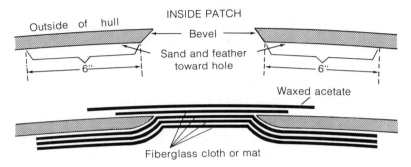

INSIDE PATCH

Outside of hull

Bevel

Sand and feather toward hole

6"

6"

Waxed acetate

Fiberglass cloth or mat

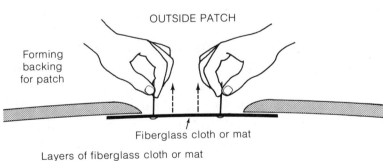

OUTSIDE PATCH

Forming backing for patch

Fiberglass cloth or mat

Layers of fiberglass cloth or mat

Patching fiberglass: cut out damaged section, then use inside or outside patch.

Outside Patches

If the damage is in a location that does not allow you to work from inside the boat, you can apply an outside patch. Preparation of the hull is the same as described above: cleaning, beveled edge, sanding. With an outside patch, however, you will want to feather the outside edges of the hole so that you can lay up the layers of cloth you'll need.

The first step is to provide a "bridge" for your patch so that the hole will be filled on the same plane as the rest of the hull and not be a built-up bulge on the outside of the boat. If you're able to get supporting material behind the hole (waxed acetate), do so. You can also try to set a mat of fiberglass behind the hole by saturating it with mixed resin, folding it through the hole from the outside, and pulling it up against the back of the hole by pulling against pins or small nails you had previously set in the mat.

Failing that, you can build a bridge by overlapping the hole with a piece of saturated cloth, extending two or three inches beyond the edge. As it becomes tacky and begins to harden, push in on the cloth to a depth equal to the thickness of the hull, allowing room for the patch. Set in your saturated mat patch, or layers of cloth, and build up the work until it is flush with the lines of the boat, overlapping into the feathered edges. When it has cured, you are ready to sand and finish off as per the instructions above.

Fiberglass Hull Covering

Fiberglass can also be used to repair boats made of metal, wood, and ferrocement. Instead of restricting your use of this material for specific area repairs, you can use it to protect large areas. I used fiberglass tape, woven into lengths six inches in width, to cover the seams below the waterline wherever one sheet of plywood met another. A neighbor of mine used fiberglass to cover the bottom of his wooden boat up to the waterline, for extra safety. You can cover your entire boat with this magic cloth, giving it added strength, a new beauty, and lower maintenance need.

Boat Covering Reference Chart

Differences between amounts of material suggested below and amounts used are due to existence of many styles of boats in the same classes. This chart is for the average boat in each classification.

Kristal Kraft, Inc., one of the many companies manufacturing fiberglass materials, has developed a chart that you can use to determine how much you will need to cover your boat in fiberglass cloth.

BOAT SIZE AND TYPE	COVERS TO	AMOUNT FIBER-GLASS CLOTH
12' less than 58" beam	Sprayrails	4 yds. 60"
12' Outboard	Sprayrails	9 yds. 38"
12' Outboard	Gunwales	9 yds. 44"
14' less than 58" beam	Sprayrails	5 yds. 60"
14' Outboard	Sprayrails	10 yds. 38"
14' Outboard	Gunwales	10 yds. 50"

BOAT SIZE AND TYPE	COVERS TO	AMOUNT FIBER-GLASS CLOTH
16' less than 58" beam	Sprayrails	6 yds. 60"
16' Outboard	Sprayrails	10 yds. 44"
16' Outboard	Gunwales	12 yds. 60"
17' Outboard	Sprayrails	11 yds. 50"
17' Outboard	Gunwales	11 yds. 60"
12' Clinker	Sprayrails	4 yds. 60"
	Gunwales	9 yds. 60"
14' Clinker	Sprayrails	5 yds. 60"
	Gunwales	11 yds. 60"
16' Clinker	Sprayrails	6 yds. 60"
	Gunwales	12 yds. 60"
16' Sailboat	Entire Hull	14 yds. 50"
15' Canoe	Entire Hull	5 yds. 60"
17' Canoe	Entire Hull	6 yds. 60"
18' Canoe	Entire Hull	7 yds. 60"

For kits below, see your dealer about cutting cloth to size required.

21' Sailboat	Entire Hull	18 yds. 60"
17' Inboard—2 ply	Sprayrails	22 yds. 50"
17' Inboard	Gunwales	22 yds. 60"
18' Cruiser Outboard—1 ply	Sprayrails	11 yds. 50"
18' Cruiser Inboard—2 ply	Sprayrails	22 yds. 50"
18' Cruiser Outboard	Gunwales	12 yds. 60"

BOAT SIZE AND TYPE	COVERS TO	AMOUNT FIBER-GLASS CLOTH
18' Cruiser Outboard—2 ply	Gunwales	24 yds. 60"
21' Outboard—2 ply	Sprayrails	27 yds. 50"
21' Inboard—3 ply	Sprayrails	40 yds. 50"
21' Outboard—2 ply	Gunwales	27 yds. 60"
21' Inboard—3 ply	Gunwales	40 yds. 60"

The amount of resin you will need depends on the surface to which you are applying the cloth, the thickness of the cloth, the number of layers, and the type of resin mixture you will be using.

If you intend to cover a wooden hull with fiberglass, you'll have to sand down to bare fresh wood. No paint, varnish, dirt, or oily substances may remain, or the cloth will not adhere. *Rough*, not fine, sanding is called for. Don't use a chemical paint remover or blowtorch; these will leave a residue that will interfere with adhesion.

Now you are ready to remove any loose seam filling and to fill in dents and gouges. Do not use rubber- or oil-based fillers for this work. If there are major damage areas, repair these as per the instructions above before covering the entire hull.

Cut the cloth to the proper length, but allow enough extra material so that you can position it smoothly on the hull. Don't trim too closely before it is set in resin.

Stir the resin and add color at this time if you are using any. Add the hardening agent (catalyst) *after* you have added the coloring. Never mix more than one quart at one time. If this is the first time you are using fiberglass, mix a small quantity of resin, adding a proportionate amount of hardener, and work with this until you become accustomed to it.

Brush on a base coat of your mixture to the area you will be covering with cloth. Flow it on like varnish; do not brush it out too much. Remember, you only have a few minutes before the mix begins to harden. Do not cover the entire hull with a base coat at this time.

Next, lay the cloth over the area you have brushed. (Always work along the length of the boat, if possible. The cloth should go from stem to stern. Avoid overlapping lengths of cloth along the hull.) The weave of the cloth is very open and loose; any wrinkles can be worked out by tugging at the ends and sides until they flatten out and disappear. Work from the middle of the piece of cloth you layed on the resin and, with your hands, a squeegee, or a roller, force out any remaining wrinkles and air bubbles to the sides, making sure the cloth is pressed firmly into the resin and has good contact at all points. Now is the time to cut and trim any excess cloth and press it into the resin.

Wait a few minutes for the resin to begin hardening, and then apply another coat over the cloth. Flow it on as before, and do not brush it out thin; this may force air bubbles into the cloth or lift it from

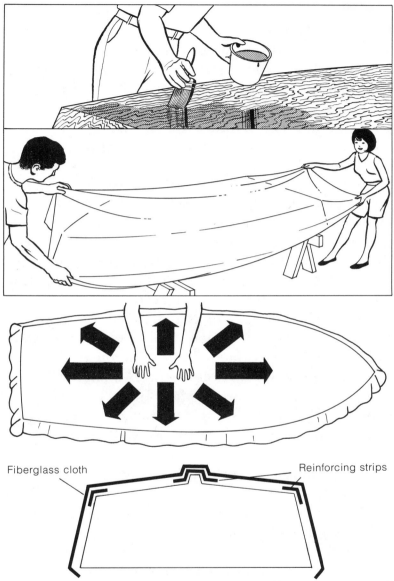

Fiberglass cloth

Reinforcing strips

Covering wooden hull with fiberglass: apply resin; stretch cloth over hull; smooth out cloth; reinforce corners.

the wood. The cloth should be thoroughly saturated and the weave filled with resin.

Repeat these steps and complete the hull. Once it has dried, you can sand away the stiff cloth at the edges and smooth out any overlaps. Sand until the finish is smooth to the touch; then apply a final coat of mixed resin over the entire hull, brushing it out smooth until it settles to a mirror-like finish.

Keels and keelboards, chines, sprayrails, and transoms will need extra reinforcement. It is better to do this with cloth tape (with woven edges) or with strips about six inches wide cut from the cloth. This step should be done *prior* to the laying of large sheets of fiberglass along the hull. Ditto for the reinforcement of centerboard trunks on sailboats.

Fiberglass will go over steel and aluminum hulls, as well. A coarse sandpaper, steel wool, or sandblasting will get the surface ready. Chemical cleaning is recommended for stainless steel. Mix hydrofluoric and nitric acid solutions fifty-fifty. Protect your hands and keep the solution away from your eyes. Then wash the surface thoroughly with water and dry.

Do all fiberglass work in a place that is protected from wind, sun, and rain. The temperature will affect the hardening of the resin; it should be above 60 degrees and below 95.

Read the manufacturer's directions carefully; consult your dealer and try to observe someone else before tackling the job yourself.

chapter 3

THE WOODEN HULL

Wooden boats are easy to take care of. In fact, all boats are easy to take care of.

A good wooden boat will outlive you and be around for your grandchildren to enjoy. All that is required is a minimum of attention . . . at the right time.

A wooden hull, well-protected with paint and preservatives, tightly sealed, and adequately ventilated, can last for literally hundreds of years. Many have. Inattention and neglect, however, will lead to all sorts of problems. Moreover, accidents will happen.

Rot

It doesn't matter whether you call it wet or dry rot: wood once infested with the fungus is useless. You can usually detect rot by the dark staining of wood or by a fine, white powdery deposit. You can confirm this visual inspection with your penknife.

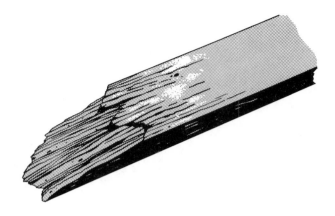

Best way to treat rot is to
cut it all out.

On sound wood, the knife point will only go into
the wood a short way. In rotted wood, it will go
in much deeper, sometimes up to the handle. If the
wood can be picked away like so much dead putty
or if it gives under pressure like a hard sponge, you
have rot.

You must get it out quick, because it can spread.
Some products on the market make the claim that
injecting them into the rot will make it rock hard,
harder than the wood was originally. This might
work very well if you have x-ray eyes and can make
sure you've reached all of the interior rot. I wouldn't
use a preparation like this except on a very small
spot of rot on a large timber. Then I'd make a mental
note to check it every so often.

The best way to treat rot is to cut it all out. Then,
for good measure, cut out some of the adjoining wood

70

that appears to be in good condition. The commercial rot killers, or simple copper napthenate, should then be used to swab out the area. New wood must then be set in place of the old wood that has been removed. How this is done depends on where you found the rot and how extensive the damage is. You'll find specific instructions later in this chapter on replacing sections of timber.

Minor Accidents

Gouges, dents, scratches, and nicks in wood are not serious except insofar as they scrape away the outer protective covering of paint. Cleaning out the area to bare wood makes possible easy repair with surfacing compounds or trowel cements. This is covered in detail in Chapter One.

Major Accidents

Any accident not minor is major. Running into the dock at fifteen miles an hour will do harm to the dock and your boat, even if it isn't immediately apparent. You may not be stove in, but chances are you split or seriously weakened a plank or framing member. After any such collision against the dock, another boat, or a submerged obstacle, the first thing you must do is inspect your boat and try to find the damage. Look for tiny hairline splits along the grain near the point of impact. Splintering may have occurred. Another telltale sign is the popping of the putty covering nail and screw heads.

Planked Hulls

Regardless of the cause, you may someday be faced with having to replace one or more planks. This isn't difficult at all and can be accomplished by almost anyone with ordinary hand tools.

The first step is to remove the damaged plank. It isn't necessary to remove all of the plank the length of the hull. Remove the damaged section and enough of the plank that reaches beyond the framing ribs by two or three inches. It is important to take out the old plank *beyond* the rib so that you can later attach the new plank to butt plates (or butt blocks). Never bring the ends of two planks together at the point where they meet a rib and attempt, by screwing at an angle, to join the ends of two planks to the same rib.

You can find the proper spot to cut away the plank by scribing just beyond the spot where the fastenings are "in line." Or you can go inside the boat and drill a small hole through the plank two or three inches from the rib. An electric saber saw or hand-held keyhole saw will serve to cut the plank away neatly. Then you must remove the screws carefully. Don't rip the plank away from the hull just because it is damaged. You'll ruin the screw holes that you have to use again. If you strip one of the screw holes, plug it up with a sliver of similar wood that has been dipped in glue. This will give the screw better purchase. If the plank has been nailed on, you'll have trouble pulling it loose. Boat nails don't screw out, and they resist pulling. Dig into the old plank and expose the nailheads. Then cut them off. The plank should now come off easily. Drive the remainder of the nail into the rib.

If you are working on a double-bottomed boat, remove the outer plank to see if the inner construction is also damaged. If it is, you'll have to remove it as well, but make sure that both sections are not cut away at exactly the same place. Cut one end of the inner plank at a place different from where the outer plank was cut or you'll have a weak repair job.

Now clean out the edges of the space left by the removal of the old plank. Scrape away all old seam compound and paint. Get the edges smooth and square to the bare wood with a file.

Some planked hulls are battened along the inside of the seam. Check the battens for damage above and below the plank you removed. Replace them if necessary. If not, clean them to bare wood.

If the section of plank you are replacing was a short one and relatively straight, the job will be easy. But if it is a long one, of varying width and with a curve to it, you will have to shape the new piece.

Use the old plank as a guide and draw an outline around it, allowing for any curves. A plane, drawknife, or electric sander can be used for final shaping after you have sawed the plank. Test the new piece against the open space for fit as you are working. The length of the new piece should match the length of the open space exactly. Don't worry about swelling along the length. The width of the plank, however, must allow for swelling or it will buckle or split. Allow between $1/32$ and $1/16$ of an inch, depending on the width of the plank.

Before installing the new plank, check the ribs to make sure they aren't also damaged. If they are seriously damaged, they too must be replaced. If there is only a minor split, splints can be screwed onto either side.

Now you are ready to test the new plank for fit in the space. You can do this by temporarily fastening one end down with a screw or nail. If all checks out, you are ready to set the plank in.

With a caulking gun or putty knife, apply bedding compound to all surfaces where wood will meet wood. Make sure that you apply enough. I've followed the practice of putting the compound both on the boat surfaces *and* on the edges of the new plank. After it has been screwed down, you can always clean away the excess.

Don't pre-drill all the holes you think you'll need in advance. Screw down the forward end of the plank; then go to the other end and make that fast.

74

Then you can pre-drill a few holes in advance. You can set the first few screws about a foot apart, then come back and set in additional screws about three or four inches apart. Countersink all screw or nail holes before they are driven home all the way. Nails can be used instead of screws, but you'll need more of them—perhaps two inches apart. I've always alternated between screws and nails, setting them in about three inches away from each other, and have not had any problem.

Butt blocks or plates are short sections of wood fastened to the *inside* of the boat where any two ends of outer planking meet. You may need one at either end of your repair job. These, too, should be thoroughly covered with bedding compound. Use many screws fastened from the outside of the hull, since butt blocks are under tremendous pressure.

If you are replacing an entire plank the length of the hull, follow the procedures above, but don't cut off the stern end of the plank until after you have fastened it to the hull beginning at the bow. When you approach the end of the plank, cut off any excess. (Don't forget to allow yourself some extra length. You won't be able to add on an extra quarter of an inch if you cut short.)

You are now ready to plug up the countersunk holes. You can use any of the surface putties sold for this purpose. Some will have to be built up in layers in order to dry properly. Fill the holes above the surrounding surface. Some shrinking will occur in nearly all of these compounds and you don't want concave depressions along your hull. When thoroughly dry, sand off flush with the hull.

A better method of filling these holes is with wooden plugs. You can make them yourself with a plugcutter from the same wood used to make the repair, or you can buy them at your supply store. They should be covered with glue and gently tapped into the hole until they will go no further. Be careful not to smash them with your hammer or split them. When the glue has dried, chip off the top of the plug with a chisel (don't dig in!); then sand flush.

Lapstrake Hulls

"Clinkers" are built like a shingled house. The plank above overlaps the plank below and they are murder to repair. Clinker boats are sometimes easier to build, but they are certainly more difficult to fix than conventional hulls. First, most of the planks are beveled—thinner along the topside then the bottom side. Next, the bottom edge sometimes has to be beveled in order to present a clean line along the hull that will conform to the appearance of the rest of the boat.

Removing the damaged plank will be slightly more difficult, as you'll have to cut *under* the overhead plank where it overlaps. In addition, you'll

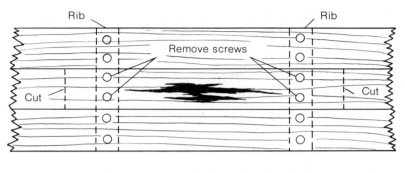

Rib Rib

Remove screws

Cut Cut

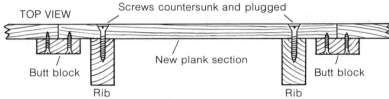

TOP VIEW   Screws countersunk and plugged

Butt block   New plank section   Butt block

Rib   Rib

Repair of Planked Hull.

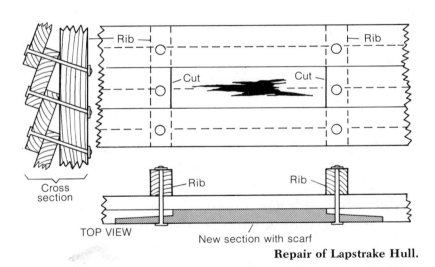

Rib Rib

Cut Cut

Cross
section

Rib   Rib

TOP VIEW   New section with scarf

Repair of Lapstrake Hull.

77

have to remove the top and bottom rows of fastenings. Clinkers are rarely double-planked, unless they've been laid over plywood. When removing a clinker plank, do *not* cut the damaged section two inches beyond the rib at either end, as you do with a conventional hull. The clinker plank must be cut off *at* the rib.

Now you are ready to scarf the ends of the plank that are still attached to the boat (unless you are removing an entire plank from stem to stern). Scarfing is difficult, and you'll be tempted to cut the damaged section beyond the rib and use a butt block, but don't do it. Scarfing a plank may require practice and patience unless you are very handy with tools and have a good eye. The scarfed ends of the planks on the boat should be at least three inches in length and up to four inches if the plank is thicker than one inch. You can use a plane and a narrow-belt sander for this work.

Then you must scarf the ends of the replacement plank to fit. And the fit must be perfectly snug. Use adequate bedding compound on all wood-to-wood surfaces, making sure that all old compound, paint, grease, and dirt have been cleaned away. Install the new fastenings along the top and bottom and through the scarfed ends of the plank. Pre-drill and countersink all holes, especially those that you will be screwing through the scarfs and into the ribs.

You can avoid scarfing by replacing an entire plank the length of the boat, or by having someone else do the job for you. Or you can sell the boat and take up chess. Repairing a broken chessboard is much easier.

Plywood Hulls

When plywood first was invented, it was a marvel. It still is. Pound for pound it is stronger than any other wood. My current boat is made of plywood and it's the best one on Long Island Sound, if not the Western Hemisphere.

Repairs are simple. Assume you have a hole in your hull the size of your fist. Cut a square hole around the damage approximately five inches by five inches, making the cut square to the plane of the hull. Next, cut a patch from new marine plywood that will fit *snugly* into the hole (plywood does not stretch anywhere near as much as planks do). All plywood hull repairs such as this one must be backed with support behind every edge of the cut. In the case of small patches, back the patch with a plate or block of marine plywood on the inside of the hull, making it larger by approximately two inches all around. You first attach the plate behind the hole by using an epoxy glue or bedding compound, then screwing it in place. Now you are ready to drop your patch into the hole you cut out, again using a good marine glue or sealing compound and screwing it in place.

Screws can be as close as two inches apart, and

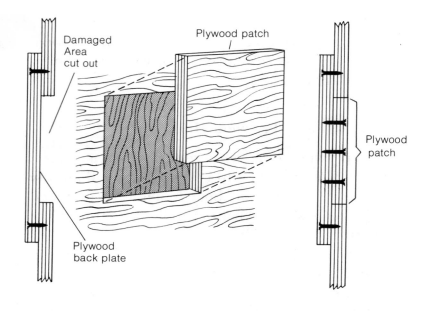

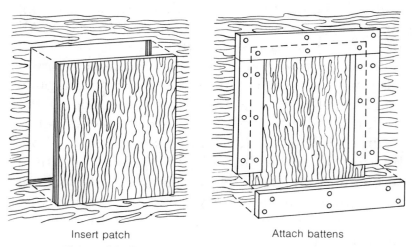

Insert patch

Attach battens

Plywood hull repair: above, small hole; below, larger hole.

you can alternate the use of screws with boat nails. Be careful when countersinking the heads; plywood is made up of thin layers of wood and if your sink goes too deep, you are biting through less thickness and you will have a weaker patch. Some boatmen do not countersink their fastenings when working with plywood, but drive them flush with the surface.

On larger repairs, it isn't necessary to back up the entire patch with a plate, but it is necessary to provide support along each edge of the cut. You can do this with battens cut from planks or plywood. Make them at least four inches wide, which will give you a two-inch purchase for the hull and a two-inch purchase for the patch. If the area being repaired is large, chances are that the hole you cut out will expose one or more framing members. Don't cut through them—they will provide support for the patch.

If the damage extends to more than two or three feet, you should consider replacing the entire panel. This decision depends on the size of the panel itself. The major consideration here is strength. Also, you might find it easier to replace a panel than to fit a large patch.

The use of fiberglass cloth and activated resin to cover the repair work is advisable. Fiberglass repairs are also the best way to handle very small damage, such as a very deep gouge. This material is worked with in much the same way as it is when repairing fiberglass boats. Consult the chapter on fiberglass boats for detailed information and procedures.

A final note of caution: don't oversand plywood. Because this wood is cut "on edge," the darker-colored grain will be extremely hard, and the lighter, soft wood will be soft. Sanding by hand or with a disc sander is asking for trouble. A rippled, uneven surface can result. Leave it alone if you can, or use a belt or orbital sander with a light touch.

chapter 4

ALUMINUM, STEEL AND OTHER HULLS

Repairing Aluminum Hulls

In repairing aluminum hulls, light scratches can be buffed or sanded away before repainting. Small dents that have no sharply defined edges can be pounded back smooth with a rubber-headed mallet. Hold another rubber mallet behind the work to absorb the blows and prevent formation of a dent in the other direction. Hammer lightly at first until you get the feel of it. Don't get impatient. Start on the outside of the dent and work your way toward the center. With practice you'll be able to get a dent out so that no one will recognize it from the original surface. Heating the metal will sometimes make the repair easier. Don't overheat; aluminum doesn't change color the way steel does when heated. Sprinkle with cold water when done. It may be necessary to drill a small hole in the center of the dent to allow for metal displacement. This can later be filled up according to instructions you'll find later in this chapter.

Cracks in aluminum can spread unless you take immediate action. Drill a small hole at the ends of the crack to prevent its going any further. Cracks and small holes in your aluminum hull can be repaired by welding, but here you have to be careful. Some aluminum alloys will reach a temper of T-6 after heat treating and, while they may be successfully welded by an expert, welding is not recommended because it will result in a brittle spot surrounded by an annealed (lack of temper) area. There are smoothing cements and cold solders that the amateur can handle without too much trouble. Most dealers carry them.

There are also aluminum patch repair kits at your dealer's. They consist of a small sheet of aluminum, some adhesive material as bedding compound, and rivets to hold everything in place. Make sure you buy a piece of aluminum large enough to cover the hole or crack with sufficient overlap. Also, make sure that the thickness of the patch is compatible with the thickness of the hole. There is no point in repairing a hole with a weak patch.

Patches are preferably set from the inside, where they won't be seen. Clean off the area by sanding and with an etch cleaner. Spread the bedding compound over the patch and rivet into place through pre-drilled holes. Any hole or crack showing on the outside of the boat can be taken care of with a filler that can then be sanded.

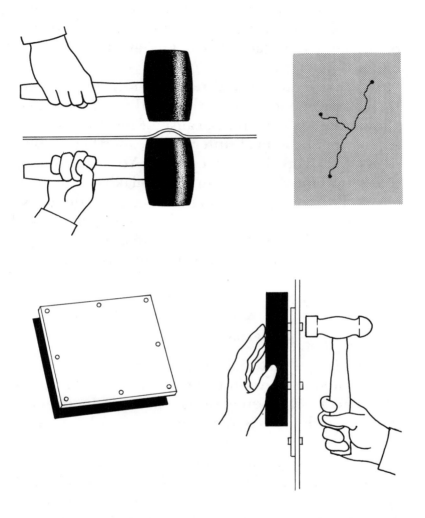

Repairing aluminum hulls: top left, remove dents; top right, drill holes to prevent cracks from lengthening; bottom left, aluminum patch; bottom right, riveting.

Hot solder, once popular for repairing aluminum, is not recommended, since cold solders, epoxy resins, and fiberglass repair kits are available for minor repairs.

Riveting is an art and requires a little practice. If rivets are poorly set in, they will work loose and allow water to seep in. Because of the stresses and strains your boat must suffer, even expertly installed rivets will work loose over time. You can tighten rivets by tapping them smartly, making sure you have a heavy metal backing plate against the back-side. If rivets have become very loose, they may have worked the hole they are in to a size too large for tightening. In this case, replace with the next size up.

Repairing Steel Hulls

Steel is the material customarily used for large boats, such as the kind the Navy uses. But more and more, steel is being used for boats under twenty-five feet in length. Some canoes are made of steel, as are many houseboats.

Minor problems, like scratches and shallow dents, can be filled in. There are filler compounds and epoxies for this purpose at your dealer's. More serious damage, such as cracks and holes, must be welded, and if the damage is very severe, steel plates will have to be used. If you don't already know how to weld, I suggest you have it done for you by an expert. You can finish off the job yourself by filing down the weld until it is flush with the surface. Hot soldering can be substituted for welding in some instances, but don't look to solder for strength; use it merely to fill in.

If welding is not practical, plates can be riveted to the hull for repairs, as in the method used in repairing aluminum boats.

The biggest dangers to steel are rust and corrosion. If the metal is not properly primed and painted, air and water will attack it. Mill scale, that blue-gray look that new steel has, will eventually work itself off the plate and take with it any paint that has been applied to it. Sand blasting is the best way to take metal down to a clean surface, particularly in hard-to-get-at places. Paint according to the instructions in Chapter One.

Ferrocement Hulls

I don't care what anyone tells me; cement can't float. Yet there are people all over the world who persist in building concrete boats and sailing away in them.

Ferrocement boats present a special maintenance problem. The wire mesh, sometimes up to six layers, over which the cement is applied is susceptible to rust if it ever becomes exposed. Builders are careful about covering the mesh and none will show through the cement on a new boat. But we are talking here about maintenance. Any cracks or breaks on the hull might allow water and air to find their way to the mesh and rust will result. Once started, it can be extremely difficult to arrest. Cracks and holes should be patched immediately.

Remove all disintegrated concrete and loose particles. Use a chemical solvent to get rid of paint, dirt, and oily substances. A brushing with muriatic acid will take off any glaze, uncured cement, and remaining dirt. Repairs must be made with the same kind of concrete mixture used in the building of the boat. The dealer who sold you the boat has the appropriate repair kits.

Trowel in the mixture and work it smooth. Sand when cured. Prime and paint.

On ferrocement hulls, wire mesh is subject to rust.

Inflatables

Inflatable boats are becoming very popular. Once restricted to use as life rafts, they are now in constant service as dinghies, as fishing boats, and to tow water skiers. The S550 Avon can carry a 55 H.P. motor and do almost forty miles an hour.

Many of the inflatables are made of nylon impregnated with Dupont Hypalon, which prevents the material from cracking in the sunlight. You can expect a boat like this to last ten to fifteen years if you treat it properly. (Some companies claim to have a special coating which will give inflatables a longer life. I have not tested these and cannot recommend them.)

After use, inflatables should be hosed down with fresh water. Spray a little rubber lubricant in the valves. If you have oars, oil the metal ferrules; avoid immersing them in salt water. When storing for the winter season or any long period, make sure that there are no small stones or sand in the boat before you roll it up and put it away. If you have space (such as an attic), it is better if you store your inflatable with a quantity of air in it.

Inflatable boats come with repair kits and instructions, but it is important to review a few basics. The surface to be repaired must be completely dry before any adhesive patch can be applied. Adhesion will not take place if any oily substance is present. Apply one coat of adhesive to the patch and one to the boat and let it dry for five to ten minutes. Then apply another coat to both surfaces and press together. Smooth out any air bubbles, working from the center outward. If the rip or tear is larger than two inches, sew it shut with a herringbone stitch before applying the patch. Sew only inflatables that contain a fabric as part of their construction; don't try to sew through an all-rubber (or synthetic) boat. Patches should overlap the damage by at least one inch; else a bulge will eventually develop. Do not return the boat to the water or inflate for at least one day.

Foldables

Folding boats are not new. The Egyptians and the Welsh had versions of "folding" boats. The American Indian had a canoe of saplings and hides that collapsed for easier portage through the forest. It was reassembled when they again reached water.

There are many versions available today. Pack/Skiff is one of the best examples. Unfolded, it is more than eleven feet long and almost four feet wide. Folded, it takes up no more room than three suitcases, and you can put it on the shelf in your closet. The sections are made of wood that fold neatly through a system of hinges and interlocking devices. The outer skin is 18-ounce vinyl-impregnated nylon. The whole thing assembles in ten minutes.

Maintenance is easy. Clean the vinyl with mild soap and water. Use a commercial vinyl cleaner for tougher stains. Treat the wood portions with varnish or paint, as needed. Keep rust from starting on the metal, which won't be difficult because most metal parts are stainless steel (which can sometimes rust) and aluminum (white rust).

Holes in the outer skin can be repaired simply with a vinyl repair kit, similar to those used for above-ground swimming pools. Keep an eye out for scuff marks that may weaken the material. Don't drag the boat over rocks or on the beach.

Other folding boats may have a canvas or sail cloth cover that has been treated to make it waterproof. In these instances, patches should be made of the same material and a waterproof adhesive used. Tack sewing of the patch, at least on the corners, is recommended.

Houseboats and Platform Boats

These are a special category. It seems that there are as many types of houseboats, platform boats, patio floats, party decks, etc., as there are books on cooking. Flotation is the primary function of these craft, rather than movement through the water. Houseboats only move to get from one snug anchorage to another, and are not concerned with speed and the winning of races. Thus, they are designed with different purposes in mind and have different maintenance problems.

Efficient and uniform flotation comes first. A houseboat or platform boat is not comfortable with a ten-degree list to starboard. If flotation is effected through the use of expanded polyurethane foam, you are relatively safe. Pontoons of metal or fiberglass containing air, on the other hand, can develop leaks, and this can turn into a serious problem. It is better to keep an eye out for the telltale signs of leaks before they actually occur. Repairing pontoons will require that the craft be hauled out of the water, an expensive and time-consuming operation.

Other maintenance procedures are similar to those covered for conventional boats, depending on the construction materials used.

Other Types of Boats

There has been an explosion in the kinds of water craft now available to the public. There are jet boats, operating on the same principle as jet planes: hydro-foils that rise out of the water and reach previously unheard-of speeds; air boats that are pushed along the water by a large propeller; hovercraft that don't touch the water at all but are suspended on a cushion of air and can also travel over land. Paddle boats are becoming popular again and people are pedaling

Newer type of boats, such as canoe, top; catamaran, middle;
slalom canoe, bottom, require special maintenance.

themselves about under their own power. The sport of iceboating is growing by leaps and skids, and a version of the iceboat modified by the addition of wheels is being "sailed" on desert floors and parking lots. The newest type of boat is something called AquaDart, a tiny powered craft only 95 inches long and 31 inches wide that moves along in the water at twenty-five miles an hour, turns on its own radius, and stops on a dime.

All of these new crafts utilize new materials in construction, and their antics on the water will subject them to severe stresses and pressures. Each of those will require a maintenance program uniquely suited to its own needs. If you should become the owner of one of these new and experimental water bugs, make use of the general maintenance information in these chapters, and follow the guidance provided in the "owner's manual." When in doubt on any subject, don't hesitate to contact the manufacturer for information and help. All of them, in my experience, are eager to assist their customers in making their time on the water enjoyable.

chapter 5

SAILBOATS

Sailboats merit a chapter of their own, because they have equipment and maintenance problems of their own that power boats do not have.

Whether you now own a sailboat or contemplate the purchase of one, you must recognize that you face a wider array of maintenance considerations than a powerboat owner. It isn't more work to keep a sailboat in good condition; there are simply more things to think about.

Sails

Sails are not maintenance-free but they require relatively little attention. How you handle and fly your sails will determine how much time you will have to put into them later. Sails are cut to operate as airfoils, except when you are running downwind, and they must be bent to the mast properly if they are to work efficiently. Always make sure that your sails are hoisted to the top of the mast snugly and that the clew outhaul is under sufficient tension. If the sail is slack and you have "scallops" between your slides, you will lose much of the force and lift the sail was designed to provide. The induced drag could cause unnecessary luffing and uneven pressure against the slides and track and, eventually, weaken these fastenings.

Sails are made of natural materials, such as cotton, and of synthetic fibers, such as Dacron and nylon. Each will require its own type of care.

Cotton Sails

Cotton sails are rarely seen anymore, but they still exist, and if you insist, your sailmaker will cut a new set for you. They are less desirable than Dacron for many reasons, but they are less expensive initially. Cotton sails have a shorter life than synthetic sails. The natural fibers will eventually give way to exposure of the elements. Mildew and rot can attack them and stains are more difficult to remove. They will lose their shape faster than synthetics and are much weaker, even when new. They stay wet longer and require more care in the storing and handling. Cotton (and its canvas sister) has, however, been used for centuries and is quite serviceable. The first suit of sails on my boat were of Egyptian cotton and served for twenty years before a gale finally shredded them. I've seen sets as old as forty years still in excellent condition (although they had been reshaped and resewn).

If you sail on salt water, a cotton sail should be hosed down with fresh water as often as possible and left to dry unfolded. This can be done from the mast, by the action of wind and sun; or you can stretch out the sail on your front lawn. If you prop it up, air will pass on both sides and it will dry faster. When sails are completely dry, fold them with an accordion fold (for maximum ventilation) and bag them. If they are to be stowed for a long time, take them out occasionally and air them. Use an open-mesh bag if you have one, or set them in a box that has had holes drilled into it for ventilation. Do not store your lines or any metal devices, such as shackles, with the sails.

Check the seams periodically and look for signs of weakness. Loose or frayed threads can develop into something more serious. Check the batten pockets, grommets and metal eyes, whipping around slides, and reef points. Minor sewing repair can be done simply by anyone handy with a needle. If the need for repair is extensive, you are better off having a professional sailmaker do it for you. You may need to have *all* the seams resewn every few years.

You clean cotton sails the way you would clean anything made of cotton. Mild soap and water will restore their appearance. There are commercial products on the market for removing tougher stains like rust, oil, and blood. Some are acidic and should be used carefully, preferably diluted, or else they can damage the sail material. Bleach is particularly bad; it will get the sails white, but weaken them tremendously.

Synthetic Sails

Most sails are now synthetic, and for good reason. Yet they, too, need your occasional attention. Never bunch up synthetic sails in your sail bag. Fold them carefully, the fewer creases the better. When bent on and furled, they should be covered with a light Dacron cover as protection against the sun (which can cause degradation), salt spray, and soot and chemicals in the air.

Like cotton sails, synthetic sails should be hosed to wash salt off. Salt not only weakens fibers but also absorbs moisture, and the moisture can cause mildew over a period of time. Salt will also stiffen Dacron. Synthetic sails also pick up stains, and these should be removed as soon after they occur as possible to keep them from "setting" in. Soot, for some reason, is very difficult to remove if left on too long.

Wear and chafe are special problems of synthetic sails. One reason is that the fibers are hard and unyielding, unlike cotton, and the stitching lies *over* the sail and is more exposed to abrasion—against spars or any other contact. Shrouds and battens will also cause wear. Some people will tape the battens

98

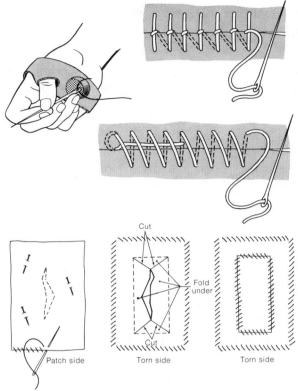

Sewing sails: use a palm thimble, top left; use herringbone or overhand stitch. Patch as shown.

to diminish chafing. But be sure that battens are also well varnished if they are made of wood, or moisture will eventually get to them and mildew will form and stain the sail. Your sailmaker recognizes where chafing is particularly likely to happen and has anticipated this by sewing in patches of extra material.

Sewing through seam layers of synthetic sails can be difficult, and a palm thimble, or "palm," should be used. Minor repairs are okay for you to do, but resewing seams or replacing panels is a job for your sailmaker. You can "darn" small rips and tears quite simply with a herringbone-like cross-over stitch. Small patches can be applied easily. There are adhesive-backed patches that you can simply press on, made of Dacron for heavyweight sails and nylon for spinnakers. Some have to be ironed on for best adhesion.

If patches are too large, they will affect the shape of the sail and cause a pucker that will not only be unsightly but affect the efficiency of the sail as well, by inducing drag and turbulence. Avoid patches if you can and restrict your repairs to sewing tears and rips. If the damage is such that a patch is necessary, cut out the damaged area to sound cloth. Then cut out a patch of the same material, making it larger than the hole cut out by at least three inches. Cut the patch as square as possible, for strength as well as for aesthetic reasons. Fold the edges under for a seam to prevent fraying. Use waxed sailmakers thread of the same synthetic material as the sail. Don't knot the end of the twine you are using, but leave a long free end on the first stitch and tuck this under the patch seam so that it will become fast when you sew on the patch.

The luff wire in your jib will someday rust or discolor (unless it is covered in plastic) and get your sail dirty. As a temporary measure, you can cover this discoloration with a long length of repair tape, but at the end of the season you should check this wire for possible replacement. When you get a new wire, make it a plastic-covered one.

Keep repair tape and a sewing kit on board for emergency situations.

Rigging

Rigging stands or runs. When standing rigging starts to run and running rigging stands fast, you've got a serious problem. When rigging fails, your life can be in danger. If your shrouds part, your mast can come crashing down on your head. If your sheets get jammed in the blocks, you could lose control of the boat, jibe accidentally, and dismast yourself.

Standing Rigging

There are very few boats remaining whose masts are held up by manila rope. If you see one, it'll probably have bamboo hoops instead of slides and a mast track. Rigging today is primarily stainless steel wire. Next on the list is galvanized steel, which is much cheaper to buy but is not as good. Then there is rigging made from solid rods of steel or other metals. These are very good and very expensive.

Check rigging for fraying and rot.

If your rigging is of manila rope, check it for fraying and rot. Twist it in your hands to open the braid, and look for white powdery dust or dark spots. An off-color appearance is your best clue to deterioration. The darker the color, the greater the need to replace it.

Stainless steel is rust-resistant, not rustproof. Check for rust, sharp bends that are a source of weakness, frayed strands of wire, and "open" twists. Test the swagged splicing into turnbuckles for tightness. Galvanized rigging needs closer attention because the protecting galvanizing can be worn off and expose the metal to rust, which can run up or down *inside* the wire until the day it snaps. When individual strands in the wire begin to break, that's the time to replace the entire length. Light rust on the outside can be cleaned away with a wire brush or chemical cleaner. Then repair with a rust-inhibiting paint.

Turnbuckles, shackles, mast and deck fittings of metal must also be inspected periodically for rust, wear, and metal fatigue. Turnbuckles of galvanized metal can rust on the treads when the action of adjusting them wears off the outer protection. They can then freeze up forever. Freezing oil will sometimes help when accompanied by sharp taps with a hard object.

Because of the importance and seriousness of having your standing rigging in top condition, I recommend against replacing any defective rigging yourself. Have a professional do it. You can buy or borrow the tools to swage your own rigging, but you'll never be sure you applied the required pressure for a tight, worry-free fitting.

Tuning the rigging is also important. The tension on all stays and shrouds should be uniform throughout. If the starboard side is taut and the port side is slack, the mast will bend. Ditto for fore and aft stays. Setting the turnbuckles for the proper tension is a matter of feel and experience. They must not be so tight as to "sing" when plucked; they aren't guitar strings. There is now a tension tester available on the market which can help you rig the boat right. After you have sailed for a few days, check the tension again and make the necessary adjustments.

Protect the sails from the standing rigging as much as possible. The more one touches the other, the more wear you will have on your sails. You'll notice when running downwind that the mainsail touches the shrouds and spreaders. When closehauled, the jib—particularly the genny—will rub against the lower part of the rigging and turnbuckles. If the ends of cotter pins are exposed, they could rip the sail. Tape over the turnbuckles where they meet the rigging, and leave no sharp-edged parts exposed. You can cover the lower part of the shrouds with a hose-like tube made of plastic that will turn on itself and work almost like a bearing, reducing friction against the sail. Such a tube can be purchased at most dealers.

Periodically check the chainplates on the hull to which the turnbuckles are attached. Look for rust on the bolts, corrosion, loose fastenings, and through-the-deck leaking.

Running Rigging

Running rigging works harder than standing rigging and must be constantly inspected and replaced as necessary. Although the most popular material for your lines, sheets, and halyards is Dacron rope, manila is still used by many people who prefer the "feel." Wire rigging is often used as part of the halyard for the mainsail.

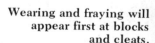

Wearing and fraying will appear first at blocks and cleats.

Manila has a shorter life than Dacron and is less expensive. It needs replacing when it shows the telltale signs of wear or rot discussed above. Once manila rope has parted, it isn't wise to repair it by using a splice. The fact that it has snapped once is a sign that it is generally weak all over and should be replaced.

Other ropes like sisal, hemp, and cotton are no longer as widely used as they once were. Synthetics are fast replacing them all.

Dacron is becoming the standard, and is available both in the traditional three-strand twist and braided. Braided line tangles less and is easier on the hands. Nylon should not be used for sheets or halyards because it stretches (although it is what you must use as an anchor line; you want the anchor line to have stretch and "give" in order to absorb sudden shocks).

Wear and fraying will first appear where the lines pass through the blocks, fairleads, and sheaves and where they are usually made fast to cleats. Breakdowns will begin to appear wherever a line is repeatedly bent back on itself. One way to extend the life of your lines is to reverse the way they are customarily used; turn them end for end. This will result in different sections of the line getting the wear and heavy use.

The ends of your lines have to be whipped or end-spliced to prevent them from becoming unraveled and getting frayed. Luckily this is easy

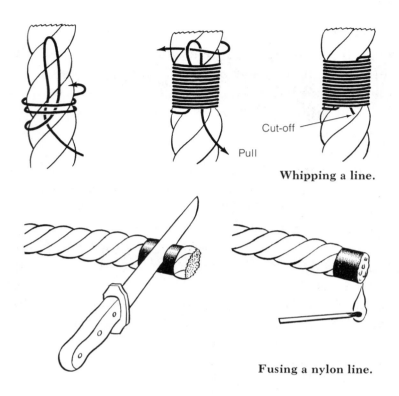

Whipping a line.

Fusing a nylon line.

with synthetic line. First, wrap a good marine tape around the line where you will be cutting, and cut through the middle of the tape. This will keep the cut ends from unraveling. Then, with a match or cigarette lighter, put a flame against the end of the line. Being synthetic, it will melt and fuse with itself. Be careful that drops of the melted plastic do not fall on your lap (or on the deck); they are very hot and can cause a serious burn. You can shape the end with a small stick before it cools, making it smooth and snag-free. You can also whip the end with light nylon twine, or back splice (end splice).

The various splices, knots, and hitches do not generally come under the heading of maintenance and are a separate subject. Entire books have been written on this subject alone. The best advice you can get is from the manufacturers of the ropes themselves. With any purchase of their products you will usually receive a small booklet or brochure advising on proper splicing and care.

Rails

On most power boats the activity takes place in the large cockpit or below deck. Sailboats are constructed differently and are usually narrower for their length. Thus, they have smaller cockpits and guests will sometimes walk around the decks. It is for this reason that life lines are necessary all the way around the deck. Life rails sometimes are made of solid metal rods or tubing, but most often are stainless steel wire affixed to stanchions.

Life lines are meant to prevent people from falling overboard and are not installed to make the boat look prettier. They *must* be higher than your knee if they are to be of help. If they are installed lower, they will only serve to trip you overboard. Make sure all fastenings to the deck are secure, preferably bolted through. Don't let rust start; brush it away.

A thin coat of oil on all stainless steel rigging is advisable. Plastic-covered wire is best.

Spars

Masts and spars are an integral part of a sailboat's "motor," and there is a lot happening on them. They carry the sails; tracks, fittings for stays and shrouds, sheaves for halyards, electrical connections for lights, wind-speed, and direction indicators, antennas for radio gear, cleats, and wet bathing trunks.

If your spars are of aluminum, caring for them is easy. Corrosion is the major worry, but not a big one if the alloy has been anodized. They can be painted (following the directions in Chapter One) if you wish. The best precaution you can take is to make sure that there are no dissimilar metals (particularly bronze) fitted onto an aluminum spar, for this will set up an electrolytic action that leads to severe weakening. Occasionally check the area near welds. Welding aluminum will sometimes make the metal around the weld more brittle and less able to withstand the stresses that spars undergo. Cracks can result.

Minor repairs can be handled with various compounds and fillers as discussed in the chapter on aluminum hulls. Deep dents, cracks, and bends in the mast should be looked at by a professional.

Wooden masts and spars are easier for the boat

owner to repair himself. Basic maintenance of the wood itself is no problem. You must never paint a mast, however. Paint will hide defects such as cracks, rot, and loose fastenings. Varnish only must be used, because you can see any imperfections through it.

Most masts of wood are hollow-cored for lightness and flexibility. Either two thick planks will have a deep groove gouged out of them and be fastened together, or a "box" will be made up of four long planks. The latter is more common. I have a twenty-five-foot solid spruce mast that I can lift with one hand, and, while it may be psychological, I prefer the feeling of knowing I have a solid mast.

Any broken mast can be repaired. Unless it is broken in two or three places or has severe longitudinal splintering, it shouldn't be necessary to replace it. A solid mast can be repaired in a number of ways. A split or a break can be bolted and screwed shut. First, load up the crack with a marine epoxy glue; then use C-clamps to bring the two pieces tightly together. Drill holes the exact diameter of the bolts you will be using and fasten them on. Do not use too many bolts, as this will weaken the member. Countersink both ends of the bolt. If the section is badly damaged and cannot be brought back together, remove the damaged portion and replace with new wood by scarfing both ends. The longer the scarf, the better. Glue and bolt as above.

A hollow-core mast with a split or crack can be

repaired in pretty much the same way. Remember to survey the screws and nails above and below the break to see if they have worked loose. Replace the more seriously damaged planks with sections of new wood and scarf these in, too. One advantage of a hollow-core mast is that you can sometimes eliminate scarfing or replacing sections of the mast, even for a complete break. Simply shape a piece of wood to fit snugly *inside* the hollow core of the mast. The length of this should be at least a foot and a half beyond the break on either side of it. Bed this piece of wood in epoxy glue and reassemble the mast around it. Clamp shut; then screw the outside sections of the mast to the new solid core.

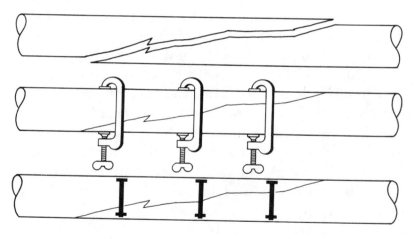

Solid mast repair.

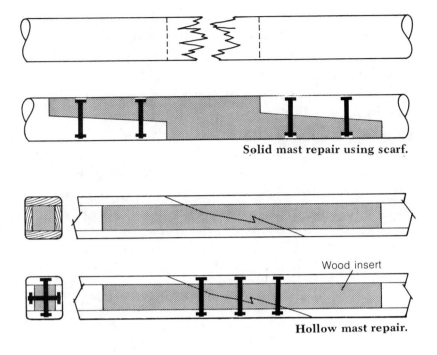

Solid mast repair using scarf.

Wood insert

Hollow mast repair.

Spar Fittings

These should be bolted through whenever possible or fastened with the newer wrap-around collars. Screws alone are seldom enough to hold the terminal fittings for stays and halyard blocks; they will eventually work loose or give way when you need them most. Spreaders should be in a fixed position and should not be allowed to flap around loosely. Wrap marine tape around the end of the spreaders where

111

the stays run through; this will reduce chafing against the sail when you are running downwind. Before the mast is stepped at the beginning of the season, check all the business at the head of the mast. Tighten the screws that hold your wind indicator down, check the terminals of the fore and aft stays, and rotate the main halyard sheave and make sure it hasn't worn down its sides to the point where the halyard could get jammed between the pulley and the side of the mast. Lubricate the pin that runs through it, as well as any other moving parts.

Give the electrical connections and wiring the once-over; look for corrosion and breaks in the insulation. Test whatever lights you may have on the mast or crosstrees.

Look carefully at the sail track or groove. Remove any obstructions, debris, and hardened drops of paint or varnish that could interfere with smooth travel of the sail up the mast. Run a spare slide up the track and try to locate any burrs or unevenness. Lubricate at this time. Also lubricate the gooseneck.

Lastly, check the mast step into which the bottom of the mast will go. If you have an aluminum mast, the step must also be of aluminum and must be bolted down with stainless steel (not bronze) fastenings. On a wooden boat you should check the step for rot, as water will run down the mast and accumulate at the step. The fit should be tight, with no "play" between the mast and step. If it is loose, use wedges.

Store the spars horizontally. Support them at enough points to prevent bending or sagging of any kind, or they will set that way. Do not rest the weight of the mast on its track or it will bend it out of shape. Store in a cool, dry place protected from the weather.

Keels and Centerboards

Lead or cast iron keels are used aboard sailboats to give them a bite into the water and permit navigation and piloting without excessive leeway. Keels also help keep the boat upright against the forces of the wind on the sails. They can weigh many tons, depending on the size of your boat, and although they "weigh less" in the water, a great strain is placed on your hull in holding the keel against gravity. Keel bolts in the bilge will eventually rust or corrode and must be replaced. (A boat designed to sail with a keel will bob around like a cork if the keel drops to the bottom of the ocean floor.) Check the bolts yourself if you are able to pull one for inspection—but have a boatyard do the actual work of replacing them. Sometimes the head of the bolt will appear to be in perfect condition, but the shank will have been eaten away to a fraction of its original diameter. Under no circumstances should you let

113

Check keel bolts for rust and wear.

more than three years go by without checking this.

Centerboards, on smaller boats, also work like the keel to give the boat direction, but their weight is not the factor it is in keelboats. Centerboards are usually made of plate steel and should be treated as recommended in Chapter One. The trouble is that raising and lowering the centerboard on its pin will wear away the protective covering, and rust will get a chance to get started. If it's possible to install a stainless steel hub in the plate you'll be better off. Failing that, all you can do is use plenty of barrier coats and rust-inhibiting paint. Antifouling bottom paint should be the last coat both on the board and inside the trunk itself. Painting inside the centerboard trunk isn't easy. I use a small section of carpet

114

about four inches square sewn onto a long wire handle. Soak the carpet section in the paint and draw it back and forth in the trunk.

Steering System

On power boats, the steering is usually done by moving the motor itself from side to side. This is preferable to the use of rudders attempting to counteract the forward drive by the propeller. It is more efficient to angle the prop to turn the boat than to have it working in one direction while the rudder is turned in another direction. On larger boats with two propellers, direction control is achieved by applying more power to one prop than to the other.

Sailboats with an outboard motor as a kicker can steer by using both the rudder and the motor itself. The only danger here is getting the rudder so far over that it hits the blades and gets chewed up. Sailboats with inboard power usually have a small prop in a fixed position on the end of a drive shaft. The rudder is immediately behind.

Rudders take a terrific beating. I've already had to replace two on my boat, primarily because I sail hard, but also because of the heavy strain and pressure a rudder goes through. Whether steel, wood, or fiberglass, no rudder will stand up indefinitely. Look for signs of stress when inspecting your rudder—broken welds, splits, cracks, and fastenings working loose. If there are serious splits in a wooden rudder, you can strengthen it by fastening cheek plates on both sides. Sand down to bare wood over the area where the plates are to go. Cover with marine epoxy glue and clamp the plates on tightly. Then screw down, countersinking the heads. Any damage too serious for repair with cheek plates calls for replacement.

On larger boats with wheels, you'll have to trace the complex system of wire rope and pulleys that moves the rudder on the wheel's command. Keep the system lubricated and free from obstruction. Check particularly for frayed wire and any sharp bends or twists.

chapter 6

MARINE ENGINES

To supplement my own experience with marine engines, I wrote to dozens of manufacturers for the most up-to-date information and advice on care and maintenance. The stack of information I received stood more than fourteen inches high. This included letters from several companies suggesting that I not attempt to teach amateurs how to tear down an engine and put it together again. It would be better, they said, to restrict this chapter to preventive maintenance and the minor repairs most people can handle successfully. Unless you are a mechanic, it is very possible that your attempts at major repairs will result in your need for a mechanic and a more expensive bill.

If you won't listen to reason and insist on having six hundred component parts on your garage floor, the best guide is the manual you received when you bought the boat and engine. If this has been misplaced, you can write to the manufacturer and ask for the Service Manual.

Despite these cautions, it is surprising how much work on an engine you can actually do yourself. Most of the jobs you *shouldn't* take on yourself require special tools and equipment anyway and you would be better off in the hands of a professional.

Outboard Engines

There are significant differences in outboard motors. The routine checks and maintenance instructions will vary greatly from one type of outboard to another. It would be impossible here to cover all of the variations in procedure recommended for the many kinds of motors made. It is possible, however, to provide you with a general listing of things you should be aware of for any type of motor.

Installation of the motor on your transom or in your motor well is extremely important. You *must* follow the exact recommendations on transom height levels indicated for your particular motor. The heaviest stresses take place at the point where the motor is connected to the boat. The weight of the motor itself is a factor, but more important is the fact that thrust, impact, inertia, and steering forces all originate at this point.

On only one occasion has my motor worked loose and fallen in the water. Luckily, I had it attached to a lanyard and it didn't go to the bottom. But I couldn't get it to start after its bath, and cleaning it out was a frustrating chore. I had forgotten to tighten the thumb screws and the motor simply walked off the transom. Thumb screws or clamps should always be on a horizontal line and tightened equally.

Most outboards have a tilt-pin bracket or device to allow you to change the angle of the motor in relation to the boat. Almost all motors are designed to operate most efficiently in a true vertical position; i.e., the lower drive unit should be level with the thrust applied directly against the plane of motion. Understand that this vertical position is necessary when the boat is *underway*. Improper setting of the tilt device will result in bow-high or stern-high operation; it will also waste fuel and cause unwanted vibrations.

Shear-pin arrangements are very much the same on all outboard motors where they are used. They are small pins of soft metal that fit on the propeller shaft and keep it in place. Should the propeller strike an underwater obstruction, the prop itself will break the shear pin and move along the shaft until it is disengaged. This action protects the prop from further damage and allows the motor to continue operation without unnecessary strain on the moving parts. Always carry at least one spare shear pin aboard.

Replacement is easy. Tilt the motor forward and remove the propeller nut and splined washer. Some nuts will have a cotter pin through them. Slide the propeller free and remove the broken shear pin. Replace with a new one, and reverse the procedure above. If you have slippery fingers, you'll want to bring the motor aboard and not attempt this repair over the water.

If you haven't a spare shear pin aboard, you might be able to make one for temporary use by filing down a copper boat nail. I once used a small diameter screw by cutting off the head and point with wire cutters.

For safety during repair, jam a block of wood between the cavitation plate and the prop to prevent accidental starting.

Not all outboard motors have a shear-pin arrangement. Some use a large shock-absorbing spring or other patented device. Check your manual.

Too many motor "problems" are merely the result of an improper fuel mixture. The gasoline-to-oil ratios are different from motor to motor and are also different during the breaking-in period. You *must* follow the instructions for your motor to the letter. Mixing the gasoline and oil correctly is equally important. You should first pour some gasoline into your tank, then some of the oil. Shake or stir. Repeat. Mixing in a separate container first and then pouring into the motor's tank will also help mix the two thoroughly. Do not allow dirt to get into your fuel containers or fuel tank; carburetion trouble can result. Once your motor is broken in, it is wise to maintain the same ratio of gas to oil from that point on, or you will be continually adjusting your carburetor idle control. Using less oil than required will cause excessive friction and wear and may even "freeze" your motor. Using too much oil will foul plugs, produce too much smoke, and lead to serious carbon accumulation.

The starting procedure will soon become second nature to you, but you'd be wise when first using a new motor to study the checklist provided with it. Make sure you have sufficient fuel, properly mixed, and make sure that the tank is well secured in the boat. Unless your fuel tank is part of the motor, look over the fuel-connecting lines and see that they are fitted tightly. Open the air vent device on the gas tank cap. If you have control cables leading to a wheel, test them out by moving the motor back and forth once or twice. Prime the fuel to the motor with a squeeze-bulb until you feel pressure inside.

If the motor has not been used for some time and is "cold," adjust the manual choke to the closed position. Do not use the choke if the motor is still warm from previous operation, or you will flood the combustion chamber. Shift into neutral if the motor has a gear system. Now you are ready to pull the starting cord or press the start button if you have an electric-start motor. Once the motor has started, you can return the choke to the open position. If you have trouble starting or trouble underway, check Table 2.

Table 2
Trouble Chart

1   Fuel Tank Empty
2   Fuel Line Not Connected
3   Fuel Line Pinched or Kinked
4   Fuel Filter in Need of Cleaning
5   Air Leak in Vacuum Fuel System
6   Low-Speed Needle Valves Maladjusted
7   Wrong Oil in Fuel Mixture
8   Wrong Gasoline in Fuel Mixture
9   Not Enough Oil in Fuel Mixture
10   Too Much Oil in Fuel Mixture
11   Motor Flooded
12   Spark Plugs Fouled or Defective
13   Wrong Type Spark Plugs
14   No Spark
15   Weak Spark or Intermittent Spark
16   Magneto Contact Points Need Attention
17   Spark Plug Leads Interchanged
18   Water Pump Failure
19   Cooling System Clogged
20   Cavitation
21   Propeller Damaged
22   Tilt Angle Not Correctly Adjusted
23   Boat Improperly Loaded
24   Transom Too Low
25   Transom Too High

	A	B	C	D	E	F	G	H
1	X		X					
2	X		X					
3	X	X	X	X		X	X	X
4		X		X		X	X	
5	X	X	X	X		X	X	X
6	X			X				
7				X		X	X	X
8		X		X		X	X	X
9				X		X	X	X
10		X		X		X	X	X
11	X							
12	X	X		X		X	X	X
13		X		X		X	X	X
14	X							
15	X	X	X	X		X	X	X
16	X	X	X	X		X	X	X
17	X	X		X		X	X	X
18						X	X	X
19						X	X	X
20					X		X	
21					X		X	
22					X		X	
23					X	X	X	
24							X	
25							X	

A. Boat Does Not Start
B. Runs Irregularly Or Misses
C. Starts Momentarily And Cuts Out
D. Does Not Idle Properly
E. Motor Speed Faster Than Normal
F. Motor Speed Slower Than Normal
G. Does Not Develop Normal Boat Speed
H. Motor Overheats

Note: Reprinted by permission of Mercury Marine (a division of Brunswick Corporation), Fond Du Lac, Wisconsin.

If you are going to operate your boat in salt water, you should remove the cowl of your engine and spray the inside with a commercial rust- and corrosion-resisting liquid.

Periodically, you should conduct a complete inspection of your motor and its fuel tank. In this way you can discover and correct any damage before it gets serious. Begin by cleaning the entire unit, including all accessible powerhead parts. Lubricate the lower drive unit and all control linkages. Remove the propeller and inspect. Trim nicks and burrs with a file, but do not remove more metal than necessary. Look for cracks and bends. Replace whatever is beyond repair. Check spark plugs; clean if necessary. Look over the electrical leads, as well as the fuel lines, for deterioration. Inspect the finish for damage and corrosion; clean off rust and repaint. Tighten loose parts. Clean filters on carburetor and fuel system.

When laying up for the winter or for any extended period of time, first operate the motor in a freshwater tank to flush out the cooling system. This can also be done with a hose pressed against the water exhaust hole on some motors. Disconnect the fuel line from the motor and allow it to run at slow speed until the remaining fuel in the system is completely used up and it stops of its own accord. Then drain the fuel tank and lines. Remove the cowl and clean the fuel filter with benzol (benzine). Lubricate all moving parts and replace the lubricant in the lower drive unit.

Now you are ready to remove the spark plugs. Rotate the crankshaft until the cylinder head is at its lowest point and squirt oil into the chamber. Do the same to the other chambers if your motor has more than one cylinder. Use the manufacturer's recommended oil. Replace spark plugs and reconnect the cables. Rotate the crankshaft again to distribute the oil. Apply a thin coat of oil to all metal surfaces.

Greatest stress is at point where motor is connected to boat.

For best maintenance, keep detailed record of motor operation.

126

Inboard Engines/Troubleshooting

You have a lot of money tied up in an inboard engine, and it is used to provide the motive power for an expensive boat. It will require more of your time and attention than an outboard motor. Frequent check-ups by you will reduce the number of times you'll have to call on a mechanic.

The first thing you should do is make religious use of the engine logbook you received when you bought the engine. Keep a record of everything involving its operation: fuel and lubrication used; the number of hours the motor has run; necessary oil and water pressure; and correct readings for the electronic gauges.

General maintenance, as with outboards, is primarily common sense. Keep rust and corrosion away from all metal parts, including the exhaust system. Look over all electrical leads for damage and deterioration. Keep fuel lines clean and filters clean. Check plugs regularly. Use Table 3 as a general guide if you do not have a manual for your engine. Although the information that follows was prepared for Mercury Marine engines, it is a good checklist for most engines.

Table 3
Maintenance Chart

Service Check

1. Change Engine Oil
2. Replace Oil Filter
3. Check Stern Drive Oil Level
4. Check Power Trim Pump Oil Level
5. Clean Oil Filler Cap
6. Clean Flame Arrestor
7. Check Water Pump and Alternator Belts for Tension
8. Change Fuel Filter
9. Check Fuel System Lines and Connections for Leaks
10. Check Battery Electrolyte Level
11. Check All Electrical Connections
12. Check Condition of Trim Tab and Anodic Head*
13. Lubricate Drive Unit Upper and Lower Swivel Pins and Hinge Pins*
14. Lubricate Gimbal Bearing
15. Lubricate Steering Cable and Steering Lever Housing*
16. Change Stern Drive Unit Oil
17. Lubricate Propeller Shaft Splines
18. Check Cooling System Hoses and Connections for Leaks
19. Tighten Engine, Drive Steering, and Trim Cylinder Fasteners†
20. Check Engine Alignment†
21. Lubricate U-Joint Couplings Splines
22. Check and Lubricate Cross Bearings†
23. Check All Drive Unit Bellows and Clamps†
24. Check Crankcase Vent Hose; Clean Hose and Fitting, if Necessary

128

	After 1st 20 Hours of Operation	Every 50 Hours of Operation	Every 100 Hours of Operation	Once Each Year
1	X		X	
2	X		X	
3	X	X		
4	X		X	
5			X	
6	X		X	
7	X	X		
8				X
9	X	X		
10	X	X		
11	X			X
12		Every Thirty Days		
13	X	X		X
14	X		X	X
15	X	X		X
16			X	X
17				X
18	X		X	
19	X			X
20	X			X
21	X			X
22	X			X
23	X			X
24			X	

The above inspection and maintenance schedule is based on average operating conditions in utility service. Under severe operating conditions, continuous heavy duty, or high-speed operation, the interval should be shortened.

* If unit is operated in salt water, these items require attention more frequently.
† See your local servicing dealer.

Notes: Reprinted by permission of Mercury Marine (a division of Brunswick Corporation), Fond Du Lac, Wisconsin.

Unfortunately, preventive maintenance will not always prevent breakdowns. Things will happen that are impossible to anticipate. The best you can hope for in a case like this is to catch the trouble early and make repairs before it develops into a serious problem.

Troubleshooting is locating the source of a problem from its symptoms.

If the starter will not turn the engine, you have the following probable causes:

Loose or corroded battery cables or connections.
Too weak a battery.
A defective starter switch.
Faulty starter solenoid.
An open circuit somewhere in the wiring.
Broken or worn brushes in the starter itself.
Faulty or bent starter armature or fields.
Water in the cylinder.

If the starter turns, but the pinion will not engage:

The starter clutch may be slipping.
There may be broken teeth on the flywheel gear.
The armature shaft may be either rusted, dirty, or lacking lubrication.
A broken bendix spring may be the cause.

If the solenoid plunger vibrates when the starter switch is engaged:

You could have a weak battery, loose connections, or faulty solenoid.

130

If the starter pinion jams or binds, check for:

Starter mounting may be loose or misaligned.
Possible broken or chipped teeth on the flywheel gear or pinion.

If the starter turns the engine but it is hard to start (or won't start):

Check your gas tank; it may be empty.
The tank vent may be clogged or the shut-off valve closed.
A clogged fuel filter or dirt may be in the fuel line or carburetor.
The choke might not be operating properly.
The carburetor may be flooded or out of adjustment.
Vapor lock or a faulty fuel pump could be the cause.
A faulty coil or condenser might have to be replaced.
Moisture may have formed on ignition wires or distributor.
Fouled spark plugs or improper plug gap could be the reason.
Check for improper ignition timing or points improperly gapped, burned, or dirty.
A cracked distributor cap or rotor will also prevent starting and should be replaced.
Poor connections or damaged ignition wiring can also be at fault.

If your engine is idling poorly, the cause may be:

An incorrect air-idle adjustment.
The idle discharge holes may be plugged or gummed.
A worn throttle shaft.
An air leak at the mounting between the carburetor and the manifold.
Damaged or worn idle needle.
An incorrect fuel or float level.
The choke does not completely open.
Possible loose main body to the throttle body screws.
Carburetor icing.
A loose distributor base-plate bearing.
The wire ends or distributor towers may be corroded.
An incorrect distributor point gap.
Fouled spark plugs or improper plug gap.
The ignition timing may be incorrect.
An incorrect valve timing.
Compression not within limits.
An intake manifold leak.
An internal coolant leak.
Low-boiling point fuel (winter fuel in summer).
A low-grade fuel.

If the engine misses while idling, look for:

Cracked porcelain on spark plugs; dirty or incorrectly gapped spark plugs.
Ignition wires broken or loose.
Contact points may be burned or pitted.
A faulty coil or condenser.
A weak battery.
A distributor cap or rotor cracked or burned.
Incorrect distributor advance or point dwell.

Moisture on the ignition wires, distributor cap, or spark plugs.
Too much play in the distributor shaft.
Burned, warped, or pitted valves.
Incorrect carburetor idle adjustment.
Incorrect carburetor float level.
Low compression.
A worn or damaged camshaft.
Improper valve lash adjustment.

If the engine has a loss of power, the fault may be with:

Incorrect ignition timing.
A defective coil or condenser.
The distributor rotor may be burned or cracked.
Excessive play in the distributor shaft.
A worn distributor cam.
Dirty or incorrectly gapped spark plugs.
Dirt or water may be in the fuel line or carburetor.
An improper carburetor float level.
A defective fuel pump.
Incorrect valve timing.
A blown cylinder head gasket.
Low compression.
Burned, warped, or pitted valves.
Faulty ignition cables.
A worn or damaged camshaft.
Improper valve lash adjustment.

If the engine misses on acceleration:

The distributor contact points may be dirty or improperly gapped.
A defective coil or condenser could be the cause.

The spark plugs may be dirty or the gap too great.
The ignition timing could be incorrect.
Dirt may be in the carburetor.
Valves may be burned, warped, or pitted.
The accelerator pump in the carburetor could be faulty.

If the engine misses at high speed, you may have:

Dirt or water in the fuel line or the carburetor.
A defective coil or condenser.
Incorrect ignition timing.
Dirty or incorrectly gapped distributor contact points.
Burned or cracked distributor rotor.
Excessive play in the distributor shaft.
Dirty spark plugs or the gap set too wide.
A worn distributor shaft cam.
Possible faulty ignition wiring.

Noisy valves can be caused by:

Worn tappets.
Worn valve guides.
Excessive run-out of valve seats or valve face.
Broken or damaged spring.
Clogged hydraulic valve lifters or oil galley.
Improper valve lash adjustment.

Connecting rod noise can be due to:

Low oil pressure.
Insufficient oil supply.
Thin or diluted oil.
Misaligned connecting rods.

Excessive bearing clearance.
Crankpin journals out-of-round.

Main bearing noise can be traced to:

Low oil pressure.
Insufficient oil supply.
Thin or diluted oil.
Loose flywheel.
Excessive bearing clearance.
Excessive end play.
Crankshaft journals out-of-round.
Loose vibration damper or pulley.

Oil pressure drop is usually the result of:

Low oil level.
Clogged oil filter.
Worn parts in oil pump.
Excessive bearing clearance.
Oil pump relief valve stuck.
Oil pump suction tube not aligned or bent.
Intake screen clogged.

If the engine backfires:

Spark plug cables may be improperly installed.
Intermittent fuel supply or dirt or water in system
could be the reason.
The intake valve may be stuck.
Improper distributor timing may be causing it.

Engine knocks or pings (most noticeable on quick
acceleration or at full throttle) are due to:

Low-octane fuel.

Excessive deposits in combustion chambers.
Overheated engine.
Incorrect spark plugs.
Ignition timing advanced too far.

Poor performance (mixture too lean) can often be attributed to:

Damaged main metering jet.
Damaged tip or bad top shoulder seat of main discharge jet.
Vacuum piston worn or stuck.
Incorrect fuel or float level.
Automatic choke not operating properly.
Incorrect fuel pump pressure.
Clogged fuel filters or lines.
Clogged fuel tank vent.

Poor performance (mixture too rich) can be the result of:

Restricted flame arrestor.
Excessive fuel pump pressure.
High float or fuel level.
Damaged needle and seat.
Leaking float.
Worn main metering jet.
Sticking choke.

Excessive fuel consumption requires that you check for the following:

Overloaded engine (wrong propeller).
Cruising in high winds.
Sticky choke.
Incorrect ignition timing.

136

Faulty distributor advance.
Incorrect valve timing.
High fuel level in carburetor.
Detonation or pre-ignition.
Fouled spark plugs.
Low engine compression.
Worn camshaft lobes.
Sticking valves.
Elevation and atmospheric conditions.
Restricted exhaust system.
Operation at excessive speeds.

Poor acceleration has many possible causes, among them:

Step-up piston stuck in down position (lean mixture at wide-open throttle).
Acceleration pump piston (or plunger) leather too hard, worn, or loose on stem.
Faulty accelerator pump inlet check ball.
Faulty accelerator pump discharge ball.
Incorrect fuel or float level.
Worn accelerator pump and throttle linkage.
Automatic choke not operating properly.
Carburetor gummed up.
Faulty coil.
Loose distributor base-plate bearing.
Distributor not advancing properly.
Incorrect ignition timing.
Incorrect spark plug gap.
Fouled spark plugs.
Overheated spark plugs.
Low fuel pump pressure or vacuum.
Compression not up to specifications.
Incorrect valve timing.

Low grade of fuel.
Detonation or pre-ignition.

Fouled spark plugs are caused by:

Carburetor mixture over-rich.
Excessive oil consumption.
Improper heat range.
Improper plug gap adjustment.
Lack of an antifouling additive (phosphorous) in gasoline.

Burned spark plugs are due to:

Plugs loose in cylinder head.
Carburetor mixture too lean.
Improper plug heat range.
Improper ignition timing.
Leaking head gasket or cracked cylinder head.

If the alternator will not charge, check for the following:

Unacceptable battery condition.
Connections loose or dirty.
Drive belt loose or broken.
Faulty regulator.
Open windings.
Worn or sticking slip rings.
Faulty rectifier diodes.
Faulty ammeter.

Low alternator output and a low battery have several possible causes:

Drive belt loose.

High resistance at battery terminals.
High resistance in charging circuit.
Faulty ammeter.
Faulty regulator.
Faulty rectifier diodes.
Faulty alternator.

Excessive battery charging is usually due to:

Faulty regulator.
Regulator improperly grounded.
High resistance in field coil.

NOTE: Although much of the information above was supplied by Mercury Marine (a division of Brunswick Corporation), it has broad and general application to all makes of engines.

The routine for laying up an engine that is to be out of use for a long period of time is covered in most manuals that accompany the motor itself. Essentially, you will be taking these steps:
1. A thorough cleaning with a good grade commercial de-gunker.
2. Replacing the oil in the crankcase.
3. Cleaning or replacing all filters: gasoline, diesel fuel, oil, air.
4. Cleaning the carburetor (or having this done for you).
5. Draining *all* fuel from the system (or you'll have shellac next spring gumming everything up).

6. Draining all water from the cooling system.
7. Removing the battery.
8. Lubricating the cylinder heads and all moving parts and spraying all electrical connections with an anticorrosion solution.
9. Covering the engine to protect it from the weather.

Jet Engines

Jet engines began as a fad but are fast gaining popularity, with more and more being sold every year. Jet boats have no propellers, no blades or protrusions. Because it is powered by a jet of water, the engine can literally stop a boat in its own length simply by reversing the flow of water. There are few moving parts and maintenance is much simpler than with conventional motors. You'll never replace a prop, shaft, or clutch. You can jet over mud deep enough only to float the boat, go through weeds, bring the boat ashore. You can reach speeds up to 130 m.p.h.

Maintenance of the jet drive is relatively easy; there are only a handful of moving parts, which can easily be inspected. If weeds or other small obstructions get through the intake grate, the propeller blades will chop them up and throw them out of the steering nozzle. (But it won't chew up rocks.)

The impeller, wear ring, and bowl bearings can all be replaced without taking the jet drive off the boat. The unit must be taken from the boat if you are replacing the shaft, thrust bearing, or thrust bearing seals.

The packing must be kept tight to eliminate air leaks. Steering controls must be snug and not have too much play: adjust the set screw on the top of the nozzle which holds the lower end of the tiller shaft. To keep the reverse control effective, test by dropping the reverse bucket over the nozzle using the controls. Then attempt to move it by hand. If it has more than one-quarter inch play, check the bolts that hold the bucket to the assembly and adjust the cable that goes to the control console.

Jet drive units can usually be connected to most marine engines. There are also simpler jet "packages" that include both jet drive and motor, which sell for less than $200.

Jet engines are easier to maintain.

Electric Motors

Electric motors are usually smaller, lower-powered units used for fishing or duck hunting from small boats. They range from tiny slave units that clamp onto a gasoline outboard when quiet is needed or when running through weeds, to ten-speed double-screw models. Electric motors are very handy as auxiliary units, giving you an extra margin of safety if your engine should fail.

Maintenance is simple. If the motor should fail to run or have very little power, check the battery clamps to ensure a good tight connection. Terminals should be free of corrosion. Sandpaper or emery cloth should be kept aboard for this use. Check the water level in the battery and make sure it has a full charge. Should the motor run in reverse, reconnect the battery clamps to the opposite terminals. If steering is difficult, loosen the steering tension knob at the rear of the bracket.

You can buy as an accessory a remote control, foot-operated unit which can control starting, stopping, and steering, leaving your hands free to fish. If you will be using the electric motor a great deal, it will be in your best interest to purchase your own battery charger.

Steam Engines

There are clubs of steam-engine aficionados all

over the world, and their liking for this type of locomotion predates Humphrey Bogart in *The African Queen*. Steamboat engines range from 5 to 240 horsepower, can be used on virtually any size boat, and are particularly popular for launches and houseboats. They are the perfect source of power in secluded areas where fuel is not easily found or transported. Coal or wood is used, and they remain far more economical than conventional fuels.

Maintenance is no problem at all. There are few moving parts, and these are easily located and attended to. Rust is the biggest thing to watch out for and lubrication via the hand-pump every fifteen minutes is a basic requirement.

Cleaning boiler flues can be a daily operation with poor fuels, but with better fuels may be required as seldom as once a month. This only takes ten minutes. Every fifty hours of operation or so, all water in the cooling system must be discharged. This "blow down" operation may be required more often if hard or dirty water is used. Never allow more than one-quarter inch of "mud" to build up at the base of the firebox. Greater build-up could cause hot spots that will burn through the walls. Repairs of minor leaks are accomplished through tapered copper plugs. Major damage will have to be welded.

One of the best sources of information on steam engines is Fred H. Semple, Box 8354, St. Louis, Missouri 63124.

chapter 7

SUPPORT SYSTEMS

Next to the Apollo space capsules, boats are probably the most complex transportation devices existing. Certainly there are more separate systems involved than in anything else their size—more than in airplanes and automobiles, for example.

Think of it. Hull, deck, keel, rudder, steering controls, engine, fuel system, water systems, electrical systems, lights, galley, head, sleeping accommodations, instrument panels, safety equipment, communications equipment, navigation equipment, comfort equipment, trailer and mooring needs, tools, foul-weather gear, and a cooler for beer are just a few.

The Electrical System

The electrical system can be very simple on a smaller boat. Batteries for running lights are the extent of it. Replace when weak or corroded. Keep

144

spares aboard, along with extra bulbs.

As boats get bigger, electrical needs become greater and so should your knowledge of the system.

Wiring

Know your wiring. Study the path and function of all the wiring on your boat until it becomes second nature to you. Learn the sizes and capacities of your wiring: wire isn't just wire. There are different types for different jobs. Inspect carefully before the boating season, during the boating season, and after the boating season. Even the best of protective coverings will corrode, become brittle, and break. Short circuits will result when wires become wet in the damp atmosphere. Look for signs of weakness, particularly at terminals and wherever the wire is stapled or otherwise fastened to the boat. Don't leave loops or scallops of exposed wiring in places where they might accidentally be pulled away from their fittings. When replacing wire, it is best to do one length at a time to minimize confusion. If you're unsure as to the types of wires, take the length you are replacing to an electrical supply house or hardware store and show the old wire to the dealer. He will give you an exact duplicate. Get the best-protected wire you can. Minor repairs can be handled with tape, but this should only be for temporary and emergency situations.

Check distributor for cracks or chips if engine doesn't start.

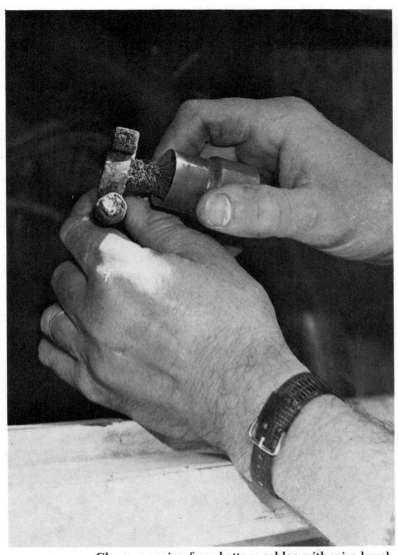

Clean corrosion from battery cables with wire brush.

The Battery

A boat battery gets less use than an automobile battery, but because it goes unused for long periods of time and is continually exposed to the elements, it may not last as long. Without it, you can't start your motor, so it is important that it be checked often. Look for cracks and faults in the case itself. Check the terminals by hand to see if the posts are loose. Clean away any corrosion with a wire brush and cover the connections with a heavy-duty grease or commercial vaseline. Check the water level often and keep the cells topped up. Occasionally check the acid reading by borrowing a hydrometer or having the dockside service station attendant do it for you. Don't take any chances if you suspect a weak cell or other damage. Replace with a new battery. If you are going on an extended trip, carry a spare aboard.

Starting and Operating System

The battery turns the starter motor over until the engine catches. If it doesn't, the battery may be weak, the starter motor itself in need of repair, cables or wiring may be loose, or the engine itself is seized (that's bad—you'll need a mechanic).

This book can't tell you how to rebuild a starter motor. Take it to a professional. The only maintenance is to keep it clean and free of rust, and oil the bearing where indicated. Check the belt or chain drive for tension. Adjustment is obvious (you'll need a socket wrench).

If the engine turns over but does not fire, do the following. Test the coil. It should be clean and dry. Replace if necessary. Remove and look at all spark plug wires; you must have a clean contact at the nipples, free of corrosion and debris. Look at the plugs themselves; clean or replace as necessary. Remove the distributor cap and look for cracks or chips. Make sure the contact points are not completely worn down, burned, or pitted. If you have to replace the points, it is also time to replace the condenser. Lubricate the distributor cam with ball-bearing lube.

Maintenance of your electrical system beyond these basic measures is not recommended for the average boat owner. After you have checked the wiring for faults and short circuits and inspected all terminals, it is best to use the services of experts. The cost is minimal, and you'll have peace of mind. Have the system looked over and refurbished at the start of the season; then rely on your instruments to help you find trouble as it develops.

The Instruments

Instruments can tell you a lot if you learn to read them right. The manufacturer's own manual and your experience will be the best guides.

The oil pressure gauge is the most important one on your instrument panel: a rapid diminishing or complete loss of oil pressure indicates serious trouble. Stop the engine immediately and check the oil level. Look for cracks in the engine block or crankcase that could be leaking oil. If there are pools of oil where there shouldn't be any at all, locate their source. If you are out on the water and cannot get a tow, you might *as an emergency measure only* try to replace oil in the engine at a faster rate than it is leaking out. In any event, you should always carry spare oil aboard.

The water temperature gauge is especially critical during an engine's break-in period. The water temperature thermostat controls the passage of cooling water by opening and closing on demand so that the water is neither too hot nor too cold. A high reading on the gauge may indicate a clogged or restricted water passage or a collapsed hose. Periodic flushing of the engine block is recommended, especially if you have a salt-water cooling system. Attach a water hose to the water inlet and let it run at full flow until the exhaust outlets show no sign of rust or salty taste.

The tachometer indicates engine speed in revolutions per minute (RPMs). It is useful for indicating a sudden loss of power or "over-revving" of the engine for one reason or another, such as a slipping clutch or broken universal joint to the drive shaft.

There should be a definite correlation between the reading on your tach and the speed reading on your speedometer. Once you've learned the relationship, you should be able to tell your speed by knowing your RPMs.

The voltmeter is the charging circuit of the electrical system. Use it as a trouble indicator. With the engine running, it should read in the mid-range, a green section on most meters. If the reading is too low, this indicates that there is resistance in the charging circuit: the battery posts may be dirty; the cables may be poorly connected; the battery itself may be sulphated; the generating unit may not be doing its work. If the reading is too high you have maximum alternator output, which usually means an extremely weak battery, one that may be defective.

The Fuel System

There are few moving parts in the fuel system and relatively little trouble will develop here if you take adequate precautions.

The fuel tank should be kept free of all water, sludge, and debris. Never leave the cap off the tank unless you are actually in the process of fueling. Keep a chain on the cap or deck plate to prevent its loss. Keep the threads free of dirt and occasionally replace the gasket when you notice it drying out and shrinking.

Check the fuel lines for sharp bends that might obstruct the flow of fuel; look for breaks and corrosion. Check the terminals for leaks. Keep the filter bowl crystal clear at all times. Never allow *any* sediment to build up at the base of it. If the filter screen has any defects or large holes in it, replace it immediately. Air bleeder pipes or vents should be so positioned that water could not possibly enter the tank or system.

Don't try to repair a fuel pump yourself; buy a new or rebuilt one if yours is faulty. You may clean your carburetor by yourself. Clean out corrosion and deposits; replace the filter and run a commercial solvent through the carburetor to dissolve any shellac.

If any water accumulates in your tank through condensation, you can remove it by undoing the fuel line and letting it run out into a container. Often water will collect in the filter bowl, where it can be easily removed. Dry the bowl out thoroughly before replacing. There are commercial products that you can add to your gas tank which will theoretically allow water in your system to "burn through." I've never seen them work.

If you have a leak in your tank, don't try to weld it, or the resulting explosion will cause a larger hole in the tank, one in the hull, and one in you. Remove the tank and get someone else to do it. (A professional will empty the tank and fill it with water to prevent combustion of the fumes remaining.) Small leaks may be temporarily repaired with self-tapping screws with a washer/gasket behind the head. Don't trust this to last, and if you use one, make sure it is of a metal compatible with the tank metal.

Fuel produces fumes. Gasoline fumes will explode if allowed to collect in the bilges. Exhaust fumes from any fuel will kill you if you breath them into your lungs. Ventilation in your engine compartment is essential and now required by law. In addition, buy a commercial fume detector that will give you a reading on whether there is anything in the bilge that will explode when you turn the ignition key or light a cigarette.

Water Systems

We've noted above the water-cooling systems for engines. The key thing to remember here is the importance of having a sufficient supply of water at all times. This means making sure that nothing obstructs the entry of water at the hull fitting and that the water pump is operating at peak efficiency. Keeping an eye on the water temperature gauge will tell you if the water is overheating.

Water tanks for use in the galley or head rarely develop any trouble. Once made of metal, many of them today are made of plastic and are shaped to fit in odd places on the boat to conserve space. There are two things to look for: leaks that can run down into the bilge or collect someplace and cause rot (and leave you without water when you need it), and stagnation of the water. Never let water stay in the tank from season to season. It's a good idea to replace it periodically during the season. Not only can water in tanks go flat and lose its taste, but it can easily become contaminated as well. Consider the purchase of a purifier.

There are also electric water pressure systems for larger boats which come in very handy in the head when you are taking a shower. Maintenance is aided by a pressure valve and gauge which will tell you if pressure is up and indicate a leak in the system. Other pressure systems work with a "bicycle pump" to provide the pressure. Light lubrication is all that is required for either system: on the bearings of the electric motor *if required*, and in the commutator end hole.

Water logging can result if there is insufficient air in the tank or bladder. Correct by opening the intake cap and replacing. Drain all water for winter lay-up and blow water out of lines.

Water heaters are a different problem. The heating element must be well insulated from its surroundings. It should have a separate switch at the source as well as a switch on the master control panel for emergency shut-off.

Not too long ago, eight out of ten marine toilets were of the manual or electric discharge types, but now new regulations designed to reduce pollution are changing this. You must know the laws in the areas where you will be boating before deciding what type of toilet will keep you from paying stiff fines. The safest thing to do is to buy a self-contained, recirculating sanitation system. These are charged with two or more gallons of fresh water and a few ounces of a special liquid. Whatever type of "holding tank" toilet you decide to get, your biggest problem will not be maintenance—they are simple devices—but finding a place to empty them.

Bilge pumps also do not present great maintenance problems. Get the kind of bilge pump that can run dry without damaging itself. Get a heavy-duty pump that can handle at least six gallons a minute. Make sure its motor is compatible with the battery-power voltage you are using. Unless you have a very old model, your major maintenance problems on it will be to keep the openings free of debris and to lubricate it if required. Most bilge pumps today are noncorrosive and nonconductive. They are impervious to salt water, soap and detergents, motor oil, and diesel fuel.

chapter 8

LIFESAVING AND SAFETY EQUIPMENT

Lifesaving Equipment

There is a good reason why the Coast Guard requires that certain lifesaving equipment be aboard every boat: it is that too many people are just plain stupid. If it weren't for regulations governing lifesaving equipment, some people would go out on the water with nothing but the boat itself.

Life jackets for everyone aboard, stowed where they can be easily reached in an emergency, is a must. Every so often you should test the buoyancy of the life jackets by actually donning them and getting into the water. It is possible for life jackets to lose their buoyancy over the years. Some jackets, even those approved for use by the U.S.C.G., consist of flotation material encased in a plastic "bag." If this interior bag is ever punctured, water and moisture can find their way in and reduce the flotation power of the jacket. The same holds true for the buoyant cushions you should have aboard (*in addi-*

tion to life jackets, not as a substitute for them). Check the straps on jackets and cushions for wear. See if the points at which these are sewn are sturdy and free of mildew or rot; see that the threads are not fraying and the straps themselves not beginning to pull away. Keep the rings and snap shackles free of rust. After they have been immersed in water for any reason, hang them up to dry in the sunshine and where air can circulate freely.

Do *not* use water-skiing flotation belts as life saving equipment or you'll wind up floating rear end up.

In a man overboard situation, cushions can be thrown but a buoyant ring attached to a long line is better. Another handy item to have aboard is the "SAV-A-LIFE" Rescue Ball: this is a self-inflating 21-inch life ring made of 8 mil yellow vinyl encased in a sturdy polystyrene shell slightly smaller than a baseball. It inflates on contact with the water. The manufacturer recommends replacing this every three or four years.

In an extreme situation, when it appears that the entire boat will go to the bottom, an inflatable life raft should be used. Inspect this periodically for leaks and repair as per instructions in Chapter Four. Larger boats tow a dinghy behind, but these are invariably too small to accommodate everyone on the larger boat.

Check your running lights every time you go out; you never know when you might have to come back in the dark. Keep rust off all contact points; carry spare batteries and bulbs.

Keep at least fifty feet of extra line aboard and in good condition. This may be useful for lifesaving, but it should also be strong enough for a tow should you need one.

One anchor must always be aboard, but two are much better. Never let rust get started on your anchor and chain. Inspect the shackles and links often, as well as the condition of your anchor lines. Take no chances; if you have any doubts at all about the holding power and strength of these vital parts, replace them with new materials. Windlasses should be kept lubricated, and deck fittings for the anchors should be secure at all times.

Use only the type of fire extinguishers that have a pressure gauge mounted on them. When pressure drops, have them recharged or replace them. Foam or dry chemical extinguishers should be used: carbon tetrachloride or chlorobromomethane are not approved for boating use. Check the brackets and pull rings on your extinguishers for rust. I've seen too many extinguishers that were rusted in the bracket and couldn't be used. Keep a light coat of oil over all metal parts for protection.

Bells and horns are required on many boats. These are seldom in need of maintenance, although the diaphragm on mechanical horns is subject to corrosion and the horn should be tested before going out on the water.

Flares and hand-held signal lights also require your attention. If the flares on your boat have been aboard two years or more, test one to make sure that the igniter and combustible material have not become water-soaked. Keep these in waxed, water-proof containers.

Ventilation ports for the engine and fuel tank compartments must be unobstructed and permit the free flow of air.

Boathooks need little care. But if you have the older type made of wood with a metal hook at the end, look it over to make sure that the hook will not come off when subjected to a heavy pull. Tighten or replace the fastening as needed.

Bilge pumps need very little maintenance, but they should be tested at least once per season. If you have a completely dry hull and have never used your bilge pump, you should deliberately bring a water hose aboard and fill the bilges in order to operate the pump and check its pumping rate.

There should always be a first aid kit on *any* size boat. Bandage compresses, smaller self-adhesive bandages, gauze, and the like should be kept in sterilized packets. Burn compounds, eye dressings, antiseptic solutions, and inhalants should be replaced if they are of the type whose strength is lost over time. Check for dates on these packages. Petroleum jelly, swabs, scissors, tourniquets, and wire splints should be inspected for condition. Keep all of this in a waterproof case which is readily accessible.

ACR Electronics (Carle Place, New York) offers a complete line of lifesaving and rescue equipment, the most intriguing of which is a Waterlight that is activated by any liquid: coke, tea, melted snow. The same company also has life support and survival kits containing emergency rations, fishing gear, flares, compass, water purification tablets, insect repellents, tools, etc. Of course, there is no maintenance required on these other than inspection for possible replacement, but I strongly recommend carrying such a kit aboard if you ever go out to sea on your boat.

Boarding equipment is essential on most boats. Rope ladders or boarding steps made of aluminum should be inspected before an emergency situation arises.

The above does not begin to cover the various pieces of safety equipment you should have aboard and keep in good condition. Sea anchors; orange distress flags; radar reflectors and the newer electronic aids that transmit locator distress signals and emit flashes of light—all these should be considered, depending on where you do your boating.

Communication Equipment

A radio is the most basic communication device you can have aboard; most are battery-operated and that will be your only maintenance worry.

Loud hailers are becoming more popular and they, too, are almost maintenance-free; the better ones work off the boat's electrical system of twelve volts and have outputs up to 25 watts. Test these occasionally on the hail, alarm, fog, and listening positions.

RDF, radio direction finders, often have a null meter mounted on them which will provide the first hint of when maintenance is required or when batteries are low. The older types operate on tubes which must be replaced when weak. You can do this yourself with a tube tester or have it done for you at any radio repair shop. Be careful when using an ohmmeter when testing circuits which include transistors, as this may damage them. Do not forcibly move knobs that appear stuck; light oiling now and then should prevent this. When cleaning plastic parts use no solvents. Water-dampened cloth will suffice. Remove batteries if the unit is not to be used for a few weeks.

As this is being written, there are more than one hundred different radio-telephones available to you in the U.S. The care required by you for maintaining peak performance will depend on the model and make you have. Generally, you should look for corrosion on all soldered connections and plug-in sockets. Batteries and tubes need replacement; newer models feature solid-state light-emitting diodes that give you a reading on battery charge. Some models have fuses that occasionally have to be replaced. The same general cautions apply to all electronic equipment: depth finders; fish spotters; automatic pilots; radar and loran. Test the equipment *before* going out. Never let corrosion get started; keep moving parts lightly oiled as indicated by the manufacturer; and use the power source appropriate to the equipment.

The Raytheon Company, Marine Products Division (Manchester, New Hampshire), further suggests waterproof covers for individual units to reduce corrosion, condensation, and accidental physical damage. Warm, dry winter storage with dust protection is desirable.

Navigation Equipment

Knowing where you are and where you are going on a boat can be as easy as driving a car on well-marked roads if you have the proper equipment and it is in reliable working order. If you never leave sight of land, you are more concerned with piloting than navigation, but in either case certain basic equipment should be aboard for possible emergency use.

Your compass is your most important piece of equipment. It should swivel freely in its gimbals. Light oiling when needed is all the maintenance that should be required. Check your compass' accuracy against known landmarks and your chart to ensure that it has not been adversely affected by metals or other magnets aboard. Keep it protected from the elements when it is not in use and take it home in its box if you will not be using it for long periods.

Sextants should likewise be stored carefully when not in use. Protect these precision instruments against shock and sudden impact. Keep them corrosion-free and lightly oiled, if necessary. The lens should be cleaned only with a soft lint-free cloth or lens tissue moistened with isopropyl alcohol.

Ship's clocks and chronometers should be checked against a known and accurate source, particularly if they are to be used in conjunction with a sextant for position-finding.

Wind direction and wind speed indicators need light oiling on moving parts and movement-free fastenings of the elements that are mounted outside of the boat. Corrosion on metal parts and electrical connections should not be allowed to build up. Ditto for speed indicators aboard; these are of many different types, some of which have rotating cables that will require lubrication.

Binoculars should be aboard any boat. Keep them stowed in a clean, dry place and where they will not get jarred and become misaligned. Keep away from water spray and rain. Wipe lens only with a soft cloth or lens tissue and do this as seldom as possible. Dust and dirt should first be removed with a camel's hair brush or by blowing it off using a syringe. Excessive wiping of the lens will wear away the reflection-reducing coating and will leave an uneven, splotched surface.

Optional Equipment

You'll want a number of convenience items aboard to make your hours on the water more pleasurable, and these, too, will need a certain degree of care.

Stoves, refrigerators, air conditioners, space heaters, salt-water converters, shore power converters, and the dozens of other pieces of equipment you may have aboard come in so many different types, sizes, and shapes that it would be impossible here to cover their maintenance in detail.

Common sense and the manufacturer's instructions will be your best guides. Apply the information above and don't take on a task for which you know you are not qualified. When in doubt, call on the services of professionals.

Galley instruments.

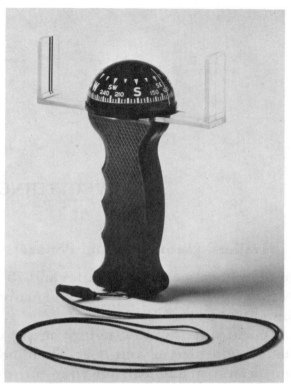

Hand-held compass for taking bearings.

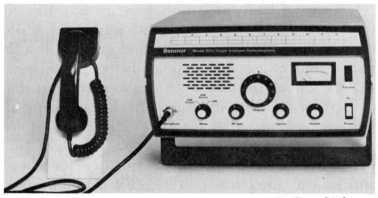

Radio telephone.

chapter 9

...AND EVERYTHING ELSE

Trailers, Cartoppers, and Portagers

Six out of ten boatmen own a trailer and 75 percent of these are single-axle. Their care and maintenance is as important as that of your boat.

First, make sure that the trailer you are using is adequate for the size of your boat. Then make sure that the draw bar and ball on your car (or truck) is up to the towing job to be done.

Check the tire pressure before loading the boat on; consult the chart for your particular trailer. Check the wheel nuts or studs after 50 miles, 200 miles, and 500 miles, especially on models with brakes. Check the hydraulic brake system (if there is one) for possible leakage. Check the wiring and lighting system.

Lubricate, with motor oil, the coupler, latch, winch bearings, lifting jack bearings, caster wheels, and power tilt. Do *not* lubricate tilt tongue parts, shackles, springs, or surge brake actuator.

166

Because trailers are often immersed in water, you should repack the wheel bearings at the end of the season and check them at least once during the season for possible water damage and corrosion. For hydraulic surge brakes, check the master cylinder oil level every six months. Re-adjust the brake lining every 5,000 miles. Never allow the lining to rub against the drum.

Tail sway of a trailer is very dangerous. It is caused by insufficient weight on the towing ball. Surging can also lead to serious accidents. It is caused by any of the following: improper or inadequate trailer hitch; insufficient weight on the trailer hitch; trailer and boat too heavy; poor adjustment of the load; rough roads.

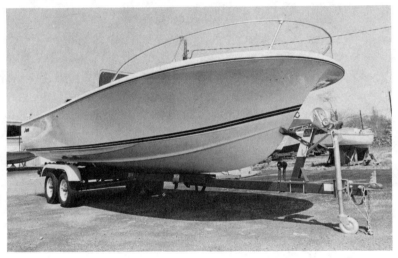

Check for dangerous tail sway.

167

Trailers need maintenance program as much as boats do.

Excessive motion of the trailer can mean that the trailer tongue is too long; that the load is not securely tied down; or that the tires are underinflated.

To keep your trailer in good condition for many years, you shouldn't lend it to others to haul their boats; you shouldn't haul anything but your own boat on the cradle—particularly not snowmobiles, tractors, motorcycles, and the like.

All metal parts are subject to rust. Treat a trailer as you would anything made of steel; see Chapter Four on metal-hulled boats.

Smaller boat carriers, such as dollies, boat chariots, and cartoppers, have fewer moving parts and need less attention. But here, too, you must watch for signs of rust and keep all moving parts lubricated.

Portagers and stands for motors are easy to care for. The most important consideration is that you must use the proper size and type for your motor. Trying to move a 100-horsepower motor around on a 25-horsepower carrier will buckle the carrier and probably damage your motor.

Winches

Whether hand-operated or electric-powered, winches and their cables must always be in top-notch condition. Any fraying or signs of rust indicates the need for replacement. Carefully inspect cabling, chain, shackles, and drum before use. Light oiling will lengthen the life of these parts. Always use a remote lanyard to operate power winches or hoists; there is tremendous tension on a cable that is pulling a boat or lifting a motor. If the cable breaks, it can snap back and literally decapitate you.

Trim Planes (Tabs)

If you have trim planes (tabs), you know how essential they are. The best type are those of molded nylon reinforced with fiberglass, preferably mounted so that they are not exposed to the elements. Maintenance consists of checking the fluid reservoir level two or three times per year and keeping the electrical connections free of corrosion.

Tools and Stuff You Should Have

The more tools you have, the easier your work will be. Power tools save a lot of elbow grease and time, particularly the sanders: circular, belt, and orbital. Planes are useful on a wooden boat, as are chisels. Files and grinders have limited usefulness but often come in handy. Socket wrenches are necessary if you are to do any work on your engine, and a basic set can be bought inexpensively. C-clamps or G-clamps will come in handy; but don't buy them until you have a specific need for them.

170

Having a tool kit aboard your boat is a good idea. It should contain the hand tools you feel might be needed in an emergency: hammer; screwdrivers; small hand saw; pliers; a wrench with an adjustable jaw; a hand drill; a chisel; and a file. You should also carry aboard sandpaper; extra screws and nails; small jars of paint and varnish; a small paintbrush and thinner or solvent; assorted bolts and cotter pins; epoxy marine glue; light wire and twine; razor blades. In addition, you should carry other miscellaneous do-dads you feel you might need, particularly in any emergency, such as extra shear pins for the propeller, or a large square of oilcloth and a means of holding it onto the hull. The latter can be used effectively to keep out water if the hull should become punctured. Place the oilcloth on the outside of the hull over the hole and nail or tie it in place. Then get to shore in a hurry.

Carry extra fenders aboard; extra line; tape; foul-weather gear; a megaphone; lubricating oil; tide tables; charts; piloting and navigation implements; spare spark plugs; extra fuel; a sewing kit for sail repair; and good detergent cleaners.

*

Covers and Canopies

If you don't have the luxury of a boathouse in which to store your boat over the winter season, it should have a waterproof canvas cover protecting it from the weather. Set this over a wooden "framework" that will permit adequate ventilation and also allow you to get on and into your boat without removing it. In this way you will be able to start work on it again in the spring as soon as the weather warms up. Check Chapter Five for methods of canvas repair.

Framework for canopy.

Canvas cover over framework.

Your boat should be covered even if it is going to be in wet storage. Many wooden boats, particularly of planked construction, live longer if they are kept in the water year round. This minimizes the shrinking and swelling of the planks. If the boat is to be in water that freezes over, it should be docked above a "bubble system" that will bring up warm water from the depths and prevent the formation of ice.

Personal Equipment

Don't leave anything on a boat that was not manufactured for use aboard. Clothing made of natural fibers can mildew rapidly, particularly if wet when put away in the hanging locker. Canvas shoes and sneakers have been known to turn green overnight from mold infestation.

Unless you are afraid of theft, scuba and snorkeling gear can be safely left on a boat, as can most fishing equipment. But television sets, tape recorders, and cameras made for use ashore can become seriously corroded and inoperative.

Insurance

Maintenance of your boat includes insuring it. Insurance will help pay for any damage incurred by your boat (or someone else's, if you hit them and are responsible). The rates for marine insurance vary widely and you should check prices with at least three different companies. Your homeowner's policy may provide you with some liability coverage, but you should check this out. Don't bother to insure your boat for more than its replacement value, even if you're in love with it. The expense is prohibitive.

Summary

Repair work can be kept to an absolute minimum through preventive maintenance. Develop a checklist for your boat and keep it aboard. Include checks for the hull, fuel system, electrical system, water systems, communications equipment, and the engine itself. Teach your family and friends what to look for when searching for signs of weakness; if they share in the fun, they should also share in the responsibility. Don't let small jobs go unattended until the day they become big jobs and endanger your life or call for expensive repair bills. Don't be embarrassed to call on the help of professionals. Watch them work and ask questions in order to increase your own knowledge.

Write to the manufacturers who made your boat, its engine, and its other component parts; ask for their service manuals. If you have a question and the manual does not answer it, write again. Marine product makers are the most cooperative businessmen in the country and are eager to help their customers. Some will even invite you to their plants for a tour if you request it.

Become an expert. Buy books on the boating subjects that interest you. Exchange information with your friends and other boatmen. If you discover a new way to do something that you think would interest others, write to one of the many boating magazines about it. Chances are they'll print your letter.

Care and Maintenance of the First Mate

Most guys with a boat also have a wife. Not all wives will enjoy boating and being first mate. If you know the reasons for her reluctance to go out on the water, you'll be better able to give her reasons why she should accompany you and enjoy herself.

Many wives are afraid for their own and the children's safety. They don't completely understand boating and tend to remember newspaper stories of families lost at sea, and this makes them apprehensive. Make sure she knows as much about the boat as you do. Teach her enough so that she could take the boat out herself if she had to, or at least bring it back if something happened to you. Go over the lifesaving equipment and communications equipment without getting her nervous.

Don't lose your temper. Many skippers (particularly sailers) panic or get testy when they are in a critical situation, and they tend to communicate by shouting four-letter words at the members of the crew. No one enjoys being shouted at, and they will not look forward to the next invitation you extend. If your wife is helping you handle the boat and does something stupid, don't kick her overboard or tie her to the anchor. Count to ten; then calmly explain the proper procedures involved in the task.

Explain that orders given at sea by the skipper must be carried out by the crew quickly and without argument. Remember that there is almost always time for courtesy.

Drinking when out on the water is a bad idea, for the skipper as well as for the first mate and crew. Alcohol will slow down your reflexes and endanger the lives of all aboard in an emergency.

Let the first mate take over the wheel or tiller as often as you can. She shouldn't be below all the time, looking after the children or preparing meals.

Give her a kiss once in a while.

acknowledgements

The author wishes to thank the following firms for their assistance in providing basic research data and for permission to quote from their literature and to use photographs of their products. These are some of the finest companies in the world manufacturing marine products, and the author recommends them without reservation. Although they provided much of the content of this book, the author assumes all responsibility for errors or misinformation.

Onan, Minneapolis, Minnesota
Lehman Manufacturing Co., Inc., Linden, New Jersey
Waukesha, Clinton, Iowa
Detroit Diesel Allison, Division of General Motors,
    Detroit, Michigan
Century Boat Company, Manistee, Michigan
B.F. Goodrich, General Products Company,
    Akron, Ohio
Northeast Aircraft Corporation, Bridgeport, Connecticut
Powerwinch Corporation, Bridgeport, Connecticut
Bennett Marine, Inc., St. Clair Shores, Michigan
Superwinch, Inc., Danielson, Connecticut
ITT Thermotech, Inc., COSOM Corporation,
    Minneapolis, Minnesota

Boyer Industries, Erie, Pennsylvania
Koldwave Heat Exchanges, Inc., Skokie, Illinois
Frigibar, Miami, Florida
Aqualarm, Inc., Hawthorne, California
Marine Development Corporation, Richmond, Virginia
ACR Electronics, Carle Place, New York
Jetco Electronic Industries, Inc., El Paso, Texas
Duo-Therm, La Grange, Indiana
Paulin Products Company, Willowick, Ohio
Signet Scientific Company, Burbank, California
Kenyon Marine, Guilford, Connecticut
Bushnell Optical Company, Pasadena, California
Bausch & Lomb, Rochester, New York
CEC Benmar, Santa Ana, California
Raytheon Company, Manchester, New Hampshire
COMCO Communications Company,
    Coral Gables, Florida
The American Telephone & Telegraph Company,
    Miami, Florida
Marine Telephone Company, Miami, Florida
Heath Company, Benton Harbor, Michigan
Bristol, Santa Ana, California
IPCO, Minneapolis, Minnesota
Columbian Hydrosonics, Inc., Freeport, New York
Caterpillar Tractor Company, Peoria, Illinois
ITT Decca Marine, Inc., New York, New York
Bacharach Instrument Company, Pittsburgh,
    Pennsylvania
Travaco Laboratories, Inc., Chelsea, Massachusetts
Thiokol Chemical Corporation, Trenton, New Jersey
Anchormatic, Kansas City, Missouri
ITT Jabsco Products, Costa Mesa, California
Aqua Craft Boat Company, Corona, California
Kristal Kraft, Inc., Palmetto, Florida

Dolphin Products, Inc., Clearwater, Florida
Gull of Bristol, Inc., Box 204 Reed Road,
  North Dartmouth, Massachusetts
International Paint Company, Inc., New York, New York
AMF, Alcort Division, Waterbury, Connecticut
Aquadart, Division of Leisuredyne, Morristown, New
  Jersey
Houseboat Association of America, Asheville, North
  Carolina
SANPAN Aluminum, division of Godfrey Conveyor Co.,
  Elkhart, Indiana
Sealand Sport Company, Kalamazoo, Michigan
Avon Rubber Company, Carms, Great Britain
Imtra Marine Importer & Distributor,
  Medford, Massachusetts
Aluminum Cruisers, Inc., Louisville, Kentucky
Grumman Boats, Marathon, New York
Jay R. Benford & Associates, Inc., Seattle, Washington
Alumacraft Boat Company, St. Peter, Minnesota
Lyman, Sandusky, Ohio
Ratsey & Lapthorn, Inc., City Island, Bronx, New York
Semple Engine Company, Inc., St. Louis, Missouri
Minn Kota Manufacturing Company, Moorhead,
  Minnesota
Electra Pal Division of Jetco, Inc., El Paso, Texas
Otterbine Industries, Inc., Malta, Illinois
Berkeley Pump Company, Berkeley, California
Mercury Marine, division of Brunswick Corporation,
  Fond Du Lac, Wisconsin
OMC Stern Drive, Waukegan, Illinois
Kohler Company, Kohler, Wisconsin
Aero Marine Company, Northridge, California
Woolsey Marine Industries, Inc., New York, New York
International Paint Company, Inc., New York, New York

Baltimore Copper Paint Company, Baltimore, Maryland
U.S. Yacht Paint Company, Roseland, New Jersey
Lan-O-Sheen, Inc., St. Paul, Minnesota
Sen-Dure Products, Inc., Bay Shore, L. I., New York
Maritime Products Company, Detroit, Michigan
The K. J. Miller Corporation, Broadview, Illinois
Zurn Industries, Erie, Pennsylvania
Richmond Ring Company, Souderton, Pennsylvania

photo credits

Photographs by Meryl Joseph on pages 12, 19, 21 (top and bottom), 29, 37, 38, 40, 45, 52, 88, 93 (top, middle), 114, 125, 164, 167, 168, 172, 173.

Photographs courtesy of *Rudder Magazine* on pages 8, 46, 93 (bottom), 104, 146, 147, 165 (top).

Photograph courtesy of CEC Benmar on page 165 (bottom).

Photograph courtesy of Berkeley Pump Company on page 141.

Photographs courtesy of Mercury Marine on page 126 (top and bottom).

Illustrations by Lloyd Birmingham on pages 15, 17, 18, 20, 24, 42, 51, 57, 61, 67, 70, 77, 80, 85, 99, 102, 106, 110, 111.

Special thanks to Stuart James of *Rudder Magazine* for his kind help.